ALSO BY THE REVEREND LOUIS F. KAVAR, PH.D.

The Good Road: The Journey Along a Spiritual Path

Families Re-Membered: Pastoral Support for Families and Friends Living with HIV/AIDS

Living with Loss

Illustrated by Patricia Chase Bergen

STUMBLING
INTO
LIFE'S LESSONS

REFLECTIONS ON THE
SPIRITUAL JOURNEY

Louis F. Kavar, Ph.D.

iUniverse, Inc.
New York   Bloomington

Stumbling Into Life's Lessons
Reflections on the Spiritual Journey

iUniverse books may be ordered through booksellers or by contacting:

iUniverse
1663 Liberty Drive
Bloomington, IN 47403
www.iuniverse.com
1-800-Authors (1-800-288-4677)

Because of the dynamic nature of the Internet, any Web addresses or links contained in this book may have changed since publication and may no longer be valid. The views expressed in this work are solely those of the author and do not necessarily reflect the views of the publisher, and the publisher hereby disclaims any responsibility for them.

ISBN: 978-1-4502-4884-6 (sc)
ISBN: 978-1-4502-4889-1 (dj)
ISBN: 978-1-4502-4885-3 (ebook)

Printed in the United States of America

iUniverse rev. date: 08/20/2010

CONTENTS

INTRODUCTION

Exhausted from years of working long hours in challenging positions, I took stock of my life and decided that it was time for a change, a radical change. Over a six-year period, I had traveled for my work: first in a regional position, then an international one. During those years I was on the road fifteen to twenty days each month. I knew that something needed to give way. I thought taking a job that didn't require travel would solve the problem. I began working part-time as the clinical director of a pastoral counseling program and part-time as the pastor of a church. While I was able to build more stability in my life, something remained out of balance. It took the process of evaluating my life during the legendary "midlife crisis" to realize that the problem wasn't the work I was doing but rather how I organized my life and gave priority to work.

Knowing that I needed to change how I was living, I decided that it was an appropriate time to follow the trend of the 1990s and reinvent myself. In 1997, I was living in Miami Beach. I sorted out options: a church in a small western city wanted me as their pastor; a college on an American Indian reservation offered me a teaching position; a colleague in a city where I previously had lived invited me to join a private counseling practice. Or I could throw all caution to the wind and move to a southwestern city where I knew no one. Much to the surprise of my family and friends, I chose the last option. Once I sold my condo on an island in Miami's Biscayne Bay, all my belongings were loaded onto a van. Over Thanksgiving weekend 1997, I began driving across the country. I relocated to Tucson, Arizona, where the only thing I was sure about was that during a previous visit, I stumbled into a monastery where I could pray.

For six years, Tucson was my home. In many ways, life changed for me while living there. The pace was much slower. I learned to take more time for prayer. I began to read, write, and reflect much more on life as I experienced it.

I was able to quickly build a moderately successful private practice using my skills in counseling and hypnotherapy. In addition to that, I also served in the Christian practice of spiritual direction: spending time with individuals focusing on their spiritual development. Finally, I became chair of a graduate program in counseling at a local university. Most mornings and evenings, I joined the contemplative community at the monastery of the Benedictine Sisters of Perpetual Adoration to mark the rhythm of the day with morning and evening prayer: times for chant, silent reflection, and listening to words of wisdom passed through the ages.

The process of restructuring life enabled me to live in a way that I consider to be richer and fuller than it was before. It was also a simpler way to live. Over the years Tucson was my home, I examined many of the things I had taken for granted, often learning to see them in new ways. The unexpected outcome of this process was to stumble into lessons about life while trying not to get lost in my own ambitions for success.

Stumbling into life's lessons: that became the theme for living in Tucson. I didn't set out to learn anything new. Instead, living life in a more reflective, contemplative way meant that lessons have been learned. They were often unexpected lessons.

One of my strategies to build a private practice in a town where I knew no one was to offer my services as a writer to several free community publications. The community newspapers would get a published author to write a column, and I'd get free advertising and a lengthy byline for essays on personal and spiritual growth. As it happened, the discipline of having to write these columns provided me with the opportunity to sort out and understand the lessons of life I was stumbling into.

This book is a collection of some of those columns. They were all originally published in a variety of Tucson-based newspapers and journals, including *Inner Odyssey, The Observer, Tucson Times,* and *Spirit and Life.* They are reprinted here with permission. The essays are my own musings about the lessons I stumbled into while trying to reorganize my life in a way that was less driven and more focused on my own wholeness. Some themes are repeated frequently, perhaps representing my own working through a topic for my own life or discovering how vital something is. Other themes are in response to issues I've encountered. They represent something of my own process of learning to live life in its fullness.

The essays are organized in five sections according to theme, but each essay was written as an individual piece. They should not be read as chapters that build from one to the next but as individual reflections on a theme.

The illustrations in this text are the work of the therapist with whom I shared a private practice, Patricia Chase Bergen. Pat is an outstanding therapist and artist. Her work in various media (sculpture, watercolor, and etchings) can be found in galleries throughout southern Arizona. She was among the first people I stumbled into when I had just moved to Tucson. Her husband had invited me to dinner; and within a short time in their home, Pat suggested that we work together. Not only did we share offices, but we also offered workshops and seminars on themes related to spirituality and creativity.

Special thanks are given to Rev. Frankyn Bergen and to Sr. Jeanette von Hermann, OSB, for their review and editing of this work. Thanks also go to Kin Lo for his work on this project.

Stumbling into life's lessons: indeed, some of the best things to learn about life are the ones we don't set out to learn. We run into them unexpectedly along life's course. My hope and prayer for you is that you take enough time to reflect on your own life to understand the lessons you stumble into along the way.

PART ONE:
LESSONS ABOUT THE SPIRITUAL LIFE

Where Do I Begin?

Spirituality is a subject discussed by many people today. That definitely wasn't the case fifteen or twenty years ago. Because there is so much interest in spirituality from so many different perspectives, I am not surprised when people attempting to understand spirituality ask me where they should begin on their own spiritual path.

I suspect most people haven't spent much time reading or thinking about spirituality. Some people go to church because they've always gone to church or because they like something about the church they attend. Others don't find that church, discussion groups, or other things usually associated with spirituality are important to them. How does a person who's never considered him or herself as "spiritual" or has never had much interest in anything "spiritual" or "religious" begin to explore the spiritual dimension of life?

I generally suggest that people begin by making an assumption. Even if you think that there is no such thing as spirituality or don't believe you've ever had any kind of spiritual experience, for the sake of argument try to suspend these judgments. Consider, at least for a little while, that there really is something called "spirituality" or a "spiritual dimension" to life. If you're not open to the possibility of spirituality, you'll probably not find it. The first place to begin is to be open to the possibility of something new.

Second, take some time to look back over your life and consider times when you had a sense of well-being. A "sense of well-being" can mean many different things. It may have been a time you felt good about your life or a time when you felt in touch with something that was larger than just you. Perhaps it was standing on the rim of the Grand Canyon and feeling in awe of what was before you. Or maybe it's the experience of calm you feel when you run or jog. It may have even been the experience of being loved by someone. What was that experience?

Third, once you've remembered and thought about a few different experiences where you felt a sense of well-being, ask yourself what you can learn from them. What about those things gave you a sense of meaning, purpose, or value?

When we begin to understand what in our lives provides a sense of meaning, purpose, and value, then we are able to take steps toward understanding how our lives really do have meaning, purpose, and value. We come to understand the larger meaning and purpose of our lives by first finding meaning and purpose in ordinary, day-to-day activities. This is the heart of spirituality.

Spirituality is not the same as "spiritualism." Spiritualism is a belief in a dimension of life with spirits and forces and otherworldly beings. A person's spirituality may include spiritualism. But a person's spirituality is primarily about life in the here and now. Spirituality is that dimension in life where we grapple with issues of meaning and purpose. Spirituality provides us with a sense of value to our life.

Where do you begin to figure out what spirituality means in your life? Begin with your life, how you live it, and how you find a sense of wholeness and well-being. That's where the spiritual path begins.

What Difference Does Spiritual Growth Make?

Walking down Fourth Avenue in Tucson, a street lined with café's and specialty shops, looking at fliers posted on walls and signboards, I'm often struck by the myriad advertisements for things "spiritual." When I read the notices offering peace, healing, and inner light, I often have a sinking feeling in my gut. I get the same feeling when paging through some publications dedicated to inner awareness.

In our consumer-driven culture, spirituality is marketed and sold in much the same way as cologne: as something that will enhance one's life. While that isn't exactly false advertising, it's also not completely true. The pitch seems to be that spirituality magically makes you always feel wonderful. That's just not reality.

By following spiritual practices, over time one will grow to a deeper sense of inner peace and wholeness. But the process is not one of love, joy, peace, and goose bumps. One doesn't move from one otherworldly high to the next. Authentic spiritual growth is a much more complex and—dare I say—*human* experience.

In the past, I've compared spiritual development to working out in a gym. When a person begins a training program, it often feels exciting. That lasts until muscles become sore. In a few weeks, the boredom of routine sinks in. That's a good time to work out with a partner or trainer. After time, at least a few months, real changes in one's body are noticeable. If you want to be more than toned and aim to build bulk, then diet becomes crucial. A diet for building bulk can be a strict regimen, balancing protein and carbohydrate intake. The training process requires discipline. Anyone serious about weight training accepts that fact.

The same is true for spiritual growth. It requires time and discipline. Engaging in spiritual practices over time isn't easy. The discomfort isn't just a matter of rearranging our lives to be serious about the practice. The most difficult part is dealing with what's inside us: the things we discover on the spiritual journey.

As we learn to really quiet ourselves in meditation, for example, it is not long before the inner shadows make themselves known. These shadows are often the remnants of hurts and pains from throughout our life, hurts and pains that haven't been healed. Encountering them is not pleasant. But working through them is what brings healing.

After more time, people break through to a deeper level of quiet. But with that also comes dealing with the illusions we all have of ourselves. This is much like being in a twelve-step program and taking an inventory of our defects of character. We may face in ourselves pride, selfishness, anger, arrogance, and many other qualities we'd really rather not see. When ancient spiritual writers talked about "demons" inside of us, this is what they meant. Spiritual disciplines require us to be reconciled with those parts of ourselves. The darker parts of ourselves may always be with us. We may always struggle with them. The challenge is to learn to bridle them so that they don't control us.

The bridling of these demons is what leads to authentic compassion. It is through growth in compassion that we learn that the pain of others is really our own pain. We recognize that the dark urges, desires, or ambitions that others have are really the same urges, desires, and ambitions we have in ourselves. We learn that while the context of our lives may be different from the context of other people's lives, ultimately all people struggle with very similar temptations, insecurities, and doubts. We all share this darker side of humanity, which limits our ability to live to our potential and also limits the ability of those closest to us to live fully.

As difficult as these things may sound to someone beginning the spiritual journey, the truth is that they enable us to enlarge our hearts and be open, truly open, to life as it is. A spiritual journey will bring us to the point of understanding that the changes needed in life are not changes others need to make but changes we need to make in our own lives. This, I believe, is the real gift of spiritual growth. We no longer have a need to change the world and make it over in our image. Instead, we can accept and be comfortable and in tune with others and with rhythms of life as they are. That's a very radical level of openness that can be very enriching. However, such openness doesn't always feel good. This openness enables us to experience both joy and pain in greater depths. The openness draws us back to who we are most deeply.

As I said, the spiritual life is not about love, joy, peace, and goose bumps. Instead, living a spiritual life enables us to live in a way that is open to all of life's complexities—both the good and the bad—and remain grounded in the depth of the truth that is within us.

Spirituality: The Way We Live

I recently attended a gathering of people for what was called an interfaith service. I looked forward to this meeting because I hoped to have the opportunity to share my own spiritual tradition with those solidly grounded in other traditions. While I consider myself Christian, I am enriched and nourished by the traditions of others. However, my experience of interfaith gatherings is that they are mostly designed to not offend anyone. In the end, they usually reflect no spiritual tradition and mostly feel awkward to the participants.

This gathering was different from the usual. The group was small, but clearly most participants had been raised within the Christian tradition. The service included readings from Buddhist, Christian, Jewish, and Native American sources. There was lots of time for quiet reflection as well as an opportunity for personal sharing. The gathering provided those present with an opportunity to consider how a variety of spiritual traditions understood a common theme. To that extent, it was a positive experience. But my participation in the event caused me to consider again what a spiritual tradition is really about.

Many people in our culture were raised in Christian churches or Jewish synagogues that maintained the essential form of religion but did not teach or impart the dynamic depth of the spirituality from which these religions grew. The result is that people today search for that spiritual depth. Some come to understand a human connection with all created things from Native American teachings. Others learn from Hinduism the many ways (yoga) the Divine Presence is manifested. The rigor of Islam and the wonder of Sufi mysticism impart to some the need for spiritual discipline. Many people learn from a Buddhist path to be mindful in the present moment and not be attached to passing things. Yet, as interesting as the variety of spiritual paths may be, many people simply learn some of the unique practices of a spiritual tradition and pick out a few things that seem comfortable to them. All the while, their day–to-day lives are pretty much the same as they were before.

A good friend of mine is fond of saying that spirituality is the way you live. How right she is! Spirituality is the lens through which we see ourselves and the world around us. It includes our worldview, values, and sense of the big picture of life. To paraphrase Christian scripture, spirituality is the way we live, move, and have our being (see Acts 17:20).

What is most challenging for us is the integration of every aspect of our lives with our spiritual belief systems. While we may have great insights and learn many things from books, teachers, or spiritual experiences, most people's lives remain unchanged by their spiritual pursuits. They may believe in a Sacred Presence in all of life, yet find it easy to treat others badly or take advantage of those unsuspecting of their motives. They may believe that all life is connected, but have no difficulty consuming as many natural resources as possible. They may value the idea of living at peace with all, yet find reasons to be difficult with everyone they encounter.

Spirituality simply is the way we live. That's the true heart of the matter. Take a moment and think about your real day-to-day life: the way you work, drive your car, and relate to those closest to you. Based on your actions, what do you really believe about life? When we pay attention, I suspect many of us are surprised at the great gap that lies between the way we live and what we say we believe about life.

WHERE CAN I FIND SOMETHING MORE?

Does my life have a purpose? Is there some plan for me? Do I have a particular call or mission?

At different times in life, many people ask these kinds of questions. The field of developmental psychology maintains that there are times in a person's life when these questions are a natural part of the life cycle, particularly when moving from adolescence to young adulthood and again during midlife transition. These are times of major life transitions when we take stock of our life direction and make decisions about what we are doing and who we are as individuals. During the early adult and midlife transitions, people often make decisions about work, career, and relationships. The decisions made at these times give shape to how one lives during the years between the transitions.

There are other times when some of us experience a sense of searching for something more than what is already in our lives. We work, go to school, and have relationships of various kinds. We're mostly satisfied about what we are doing with our lives and aren't really looking to make major changes. Yet we want something more than what is there. We want our lives to mean something, to have a sense of purpose. We want to belong to or be a part of something that's bigger than just ourselves. This "more than" dimension of life is the transcendent aspiration that is often called spirituality.

At times when we are looking for ways to respond to the desire to fulfill the transcendent, "more than" dimension of life, we may find that we begin to struggle more and more frantically for answers. We read books, attend classes, and try to find answers that are right for us. Sometimes, people who call themselves "spiritual teachers" of one sort or another are more than willing to provide an answer as long as we do it their way. Yet, in the end, the resolutions of our transcendent aspirations are deeply personal and unique. No other person can provide us with answers. Those who provide authentic assistance help us find our own way.

At times when I've wondered about my life and what I am doing, I've learned that the last thing to do is to become frantic and be stressed about it. Instead, it is important to stop and take time in quiet solitude and listen to what's really going on inside. Taking time to be quiet and listen to what our hearts are telling us is very difficult because our lives are fast-paced and filled with lots of noise. Yet we learn more about ourselves in silence than by talking, reading, or doing things.

Making the time and finding a place to be quiet on a regular basis helps us understand what's happening inside of us. But just spending time alone and silent in itself doesn't provide the answers to our questions. Instead, once we've become comfortable in the silence, it's valuable for us to reflect on our past. We need to remember those times in our lives when we felt a sense of being "spiritually connected." Often we describe such experiences differently. Perhaps we've had a sense of being whole in ourselves, at one with the universe, or in the presence of God. Remember those times and think about what was happening. It's often helpful to write down all that we can remember about those moments in our life in a notebook and then read through them at a later time to understand if there is a pattern to them.

The foundation of our sense of meaning and purpose in life is already within us. Most of us have had experiences of it in the past. When we take time to listen to our hearts in silence and then reflect on the spiritual moments from our past, we arrive at a much better place to understand the way we need to journey into our future. Understanding life's meaning is often a matter of paying close attention to our past before heading into our future.

BEING SPIRITUAL ...
NOT DOING SPIRITUAL THINGS

Introductions in a group are usually pretty routine things. Everyone takes their turn, says their name and something about themselves. Most of the time, what people say about themselves is easy to forget. It's only after further discussion in a group that most of us get to know the others.

At a particular seminar I facilitated, the introduction of one of the participants caught me off guard. She was an older woman, perhaps in her seventies. She had come to the workshop as a companion to a younger friend. Each of us introduced ourselves and said what kind of work we did. When it was her turn, she spoke in a quiet but strong voice: "My name is Mary. My work is done now. The only thing worth my attention is being something beautiful for God." Not surprisingly, there was a prolonged pause before the next person spoke.

The people gathered for the workshop were individuals who worked in the area of spiritual development. Mary's comments weren't totally out of context given the nature of the group. Yet even those of us who are comfortable talking about spirituality were caught off guard.

Most of us are focused on what we do. We introduce ourselves in relationship to our professions. We are administrators, customer service representatives, students, systems analysts, and so forth. Our identities are deeply tied to our work.

Our spiritual lives are often closely related to what we do. We describe our spirituality in terms of our spiritual practices. Just a few evenings ago, I had dinner with a few people who were talking about spiritual things. Each one talked about what technique they used for meditation. When one man spoke to me, he wanted to know what school of meditation I followed. Of course, with my sense of humor, I couldn't help but respond, "Any one that keeps me awake and allows me to sit in a comfortable position!"

Life in our world is focused on doing. We are measured by the work we do, the places we go, and the groups to which we belong. But what about being? What about being a good person who cares about others? Does that have any value in our society?

What happens when our spiritual lives are focused on doing? When our spiritual lives are focused on doing, we miss the point. In our consumer-driven culture, the purpose of spiritual practices is often to obtain certain benefits, like peace of mind, a sense of purpose, or simply relaxation. Some people engage in all sorts of practices simply to have an experience. Those are the secondary benefits of spiritual practices; they are not the point of engaging in any spiritual practice.

The reason to pray, meditate, journal, reflect, and learn about spirituality is simply to become a better person. Exploring and developing the spiritual dimension of life helps us to become the best person we can be. A healthy spiritual life should enable a person to be more caring and compassionate to others and our world as a whole. A well-founded spiritual life should help a person move past our inner pain to have a larger heart that welcomes and respects others. A balanced spiritual life should allow that divine spark in each of us to shine so that others can see it and experience goodness in us.

In the end, it's not about spiritual "doings" but spiritual "beings." Spirituality, when it's integrated in our lives, should simply help us to be better people. Mary knew what it was about. In her gentle wisdom, she was able to simply name it so that we all could be reminded of what's really important.

Walking a Sacred Path

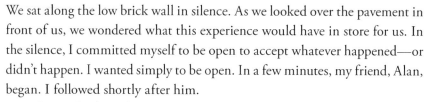

We sat along the low brick wall in silence. As we looked over the pavement in front of us, we wondered what this experience would have in store for us. In the silence, I committed myself to be open to accept whatever happened—or didn't happen. I wanted simply to be open. In a few minutes, my friend, Alan, began. I followed shortly after him.

Alan and I have known each other since the early 1980s. As friends, confidants, and colleagues, we've shared many things over the years. We had recently realized that as close as I have been to Alan, he and I had never lived in the same city. We met while working on a project together.

As we walked the winding path separately yet together, sometimes we were beside each other; sometimes I followed Alan; sometimes he followed me; and sometimes our paths went in separate directions. For both of us, this was the first time walking a labyrinth. It was a surprising and powerful experience for us both.

A labyrinth is a geometric pattern used since ancient times for spiritual purposes. Labyrinths are found in many great spiritual traditions, including the Jewish Kabala, the Tohono O'Odham *Man in the Maze*, and medieval European Christianity. Some of the oldest surviving labyrinth designs, dating from 1300 BCE, are from the ancient civilizations of Syria, Greece, and Egypt. The labyrinth we walked was patterned after one found in the Chartres Cathedral in France. The patterns of labyrinths are reflections of ancient understandings of cosmology.

The labyrinth we walked is somewhat like a spiral pattern. One enters from the west facing the east and moves along a clearly marked path that spirals back and forth through each quadrant of the circular pattern. The path leads to the center, where one may stop and reflect before retracing one's steps back out of the labyrinth.

Walking a labyrinth is a powerful spiritual tool. The actual walking is a metaphor for our life journey, taking each step along the path of our lives. Walking the labyrinth is often a very centering experience. Used to the pace and noise of our day-to-day lives, our steady walking of the labyrinth slows us down and allows being quiet inside. The walking of the labyrinth's path allows a person to let go of excess psychic energy and move to a deeper level of quiet inside of self.

What happens while walking a labyrinth? That very much depends on the person walking. Many people experience renewed wholeness, inner healing, or release of emotions. Walking the path in silence often leads a person to new insights or realizations about self. The labyrinth journey is often one of letting go of what needs to be put behind. But just as mysteriously as the path to the labyrinth's center is a process of letting go, walking back out is often a path of integration.

My time walking the labyrinth with Alan was an important experience and enabled me to get in touch with anger over past hurts. As I walked, anger I was not conscious of, including anger at the loss of so many friends due to HIV/AIDS and personal hurts by others, came to my awareness. Reaching the center, I was able to stand quietly for a few moments and let go of this anger in a way I had not done before. It was as though some tension inside of me melted as I exhaled deeply. Each step seemed to bring an inner sense of calm and lightness as a result of releasing the tension of difficult emotions from past events. Walking back out of the labyrinth provided the peace and healing to reintegrate the past hurts. When I completed the walk, it was as though there was a lightness to my step to match the peace deep within. This slow, meditative walk was an experience of healing.

Walking the circles of a labyrinth, letting go of what limits us while also integrating a new sense of wholeness, is perhaps among the most reflective metaphors of the spiritual journey. On this journey, we spiral downward into the core of self, revisiting aspects of ourselves and our lives with deeper perspective. The path isn't direct or linear. Yet progress is made by circling around the various aspects of our lives, which is both a healing process and a process of integration. That is the nature of a spiritual path.

Singing for Wholeness

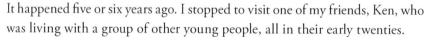

It happened five or six years ago. I stopped to visit one of my friends, Ken, who was living with a group of other young people, all in their early twenties.

As he often did, Ken said to me, "Hey, I have something I want you to hear." Ken had discovered some new music that he was into and wanted me to listen to it. As he put the CD in the player, he looked over his shoulder and said, "This is really cool. You'll like it." In a moment, the sounds of synthesized Gregorian chant came from the CD player. "You have this kind of stuff, don't you?" Ken asked.

"Yeah," I said. "And I can sing it, too."

One of Ken's friends looked at me with starry eyes, punctuating the moment with a jaw-dropping "Wow!"

Over the last few years, medieval chant has grown in popularity. While classical listeners are familiar with ensembles like *Anonymous 4* and *Sequencia*, younger people include synthesized versions of chant in their CD collections.

Many people find listening to Gregorian, Russian, and other forms of medieval chant relaxing and centering. It helps them step out of the pace of life and experience a sense of wholeness and well-being. While listening to chant has clear benefits for many people, it's the actual singing of chant that impacts a person's life in profound ways.

Western chant was developed primarily in monasteries. The proper singing of chant is an exercise in controlled breathing that paces one's heart rate. As a person sings the repetitive pattern of chant, brain waves and heart rate move to patterns consonant with trance states. This practice opens an individual to experiences of ecstasy.

The sacred singing of chant is preserved in monasteries around the world. During the years I lived in Tucson, each morning and evening, I joined the community at the Monastery of the Benedictine Sisters of Perpetual Adoration for this ancient spiritual practice. Open to the public, the morning prayer of praise known as Lauds and the evening prayer of quiet rest, Vespers, provide the opportunity to join in the ancient discipline of chant.

At both times of prayer in this monastery, a modern, inclusive, poetic translation of the Hebrew psalms is chanted, followed with moments for silent meditation. Slow, reflective readings from Christian scriptures or the writings of mystics are also included. While these morning and evening gatherings are brief, lasting about thirty minutes each, they offer a profound rhythm for spiritual growth and development.

Praying in this way throughout the day is known in the Christian mystical tradition as the sanctification of time. The rhythm of chant and meditation helps an individual be mindful of the Sacred Presence throughout the day. This spiritual practice keeps one focused on appreciating the fullness of the gift of life and helps the spiritual seeker to explore the depths of Spirit in life.

Chanting and singing are very ancient spiritual practices. While the practices are very old, each generation has the opportunity to encounter the practice as something new. That's what Ken discovered with the recording of synthesized chant. That is also what I discover when I join others to chant the ancient prayers.

Making Sense of Religion and Spirituality

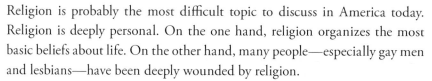

Religion is probably the most difficult topic to discuss in America today. Religion is deeply personal. On the one hand, religion organizes the most basic beliefs about life. On the other hand, many people—especially gay men and lesbians—have been deeply wounded by religion.

Today, there are many churches that openly welcome and support people as they travel along a spiritual path. That is very affirming, especially for those who understand their spiritual lives in terms of religion. But many people find it difficult to reconcile church life with their personal experience.

Even though I've been an ordained minister for thirty years, the difficulty many people have today with churches makes sense to me. In fact, I have some of the same difficulties with churches. From my perspective, communities of faith in the Judeo-Christian tradition have often failed people and, at times, oppressed them. In an attempt to clearly articulate theology, Western religion has often trampled over the experiences of the Sacred that people find most valid for themselves. A lot of religious folks are busier defining terms and doctrines than experiencing the Holy and empowering people to share that experience. In many churches, if you don't believe the "right way," then you are labeled as having something wrong with you.

I suspect that one of the reasons Eastern religions and indigenous traditions are popular today is because in those traditions spiritual experience comes first. An individual first learns to meditate or participate in a ceremony or ritual that is spiritually powerful for them. It's only after a person has a certain level of spiritual development that more formal instruction may occur. In Western religion, the first things a person encounters are the rules and dogma. Only a few believers, who make significant efforts to learn, are introduced to the riches of the mystical traditions preserved within Christianity and Judaism.

The context in which many people begin to learn about spirituality is twelve-step programs. As spiritual programs, twelve-step groups empower sobriety through a relationship to a Higher Power that is comfortable and strengthening for the individual. In the context of a relationship with this kind of Higher Power, a person takes an inventory of life events with the intent of making amends for past actions. Through this process, the Higher Power unconditionally accepts the person as the person is.

The role of a Higher Power in twelve-step programs is an important paradigm for spiritual growth. There is a fundamental relationship in this paradigm between the individual and a Sacred Presence that is unconditionally affirming and supportive, especially in the face of one's personal failures.

Perhaps I'm fortunate. Having been nurtured by the works of some of the mystical writers of the Christian tradition, my primary reference for faith and spiritual development has been an experience of Divine Presence that's somewhat similar to a twelve-step experience of an inner awakening. I learned about dogma and doctrine later and have considered them to have much less importance when compared to my experience of the Divine. It was through the mystics that I came to understand that our lives are the reflection of Divinity; that the cosmos is knit together by a sacred web; and that our lives are meant to be lived fully, filled with purpose and meaning.

Whether it's in the context of religion, a twelve-step group, a healing circle, or some other spiritually based gathering, authentic spiritual growth occurs when an individual takes responsibility for his/her own growth. No one can do it for another. As people take responsibility for personal spiritual growth, they also come to an understanding of spirituality, faith, or a Divine Presence. People's understanding and awareness of spirituality or a Divine Presence is something that has to make sense to them. That's what twelve-step people do when they identify a Higher Power. Having taken responsibility for one's own spiritual growth and having come to at least a basic understanding of what spirituality, faith, or a Divine Presence means to that person, an individual is in the position to begin the real work required in spiritual growth.

Religion and spirituality are not the same thing. Religion is the practice of a faith tradition based on a historic understanding of a spiritual presence. Sadly, the historic understanding of the spiritual presence that is the basis for

What's Important About the Bible?

I recently went out for an evening with a friend and her coworkers. It was fun to go out with a group of new people for a movie and dinner. However, when I go out with people I don't know, I'm not sure what to tell them about my professional life. When new people find out that I'm a psychologist, they assume that I'm analyzing their every action. On the other hand, when they find out I'm a minister, they think they should be on their best behavior because I'm present. Either option is a surefire way to kill a fun evening for me—and for them!

It wasn't surprising to me that the dinner conversation turned to religion. But how we got there was a real leap. The conversation skidded from the local casino, to fun spots in Vegas, and on to lotteries. In the middle of the discussion, someone asked, "Doesn't the Bible say it's wrong to gamble?" I just smiled and said, "Well, probably so." One of the people at the table was from Saudi Arabia. He explained that in Islam, it's wrong to take money you don't earn, including either gambling or interest on a loan. I explained that the Biblical prohibition on loaning money at interest is much clearer than against gambling, but the same basic prohibitions existed. "Why do we have banks?" someone then asked. I sipped my cocktail and remarked, "It's the same reason that we eat pork and shellfish, that men get haircuts, and that most of our clothing is made of blended fibers. All those things are prohibited in the Bible, too. But in religious culture today, these things just don't carry the same significance as they did in ancient times." Exasperated, another person sighed, "Religion just doesn't make any sense!"

Many people share the exasperation expressed in this comment. It is tragic but true that the Bible is the most misused text in history. With televangelists and other preachers quoting one passage after another, often out of context, the significant message of the Bible is often lost in a glut of misleading factoids.

It's important to remember that the Bible was written over a thousand-year period. Stories of the Bible represent a history of more than 4,000 years. The most recent writings in the Bible were composed almost 2,000 years ago. In short, the Bible was written in languages only scholars understand, in several cultures significantly different from the contemporary world, and by people representing several different classes, races, and worldviews. I believe that the Bible is inspired and inspiring because it is primarily a record of how people understood their encounters with the Divine in their very real lives. The Bible is not a magic book containing cryptic secrets. Nor is it written in the contemporary style of newspapers. It was not written in English at the grade level of most American publications. It is a collection of historic and cultural understandings of faith preserved for generations by people whose spiritual lives were important to them. Its significance is best understood when studied within the context of the original cultural and historic setting.

What do Biblical scholars generally believe to be true about the Bible? Simply that it is a record of people's understanding of the presence of God at work in their lives. The first rule of Biblical interpretation is that often-repeated concepts and phrases are more important than those that only occur once or twice and are ambiguous. In other words, because the Bible talks about God being faithful and defines God as love over and over again, that's very important. On the other hand, it's not particularly significant that the deuterocanonical book of Tobit records that Tobit's dog's tail wagged.

My point: remember the important stuff and beware of those who take minor things out of context. The message of the Bible is about people finding hope, wholeness, fulfillment, and abundance because of their spiritual lives. Most every rule in the Bible was broken by people the Bible considers heroes. The rules aren't the important part. Faith in and hope for the future is what it's about.

While I believe the Bible is an inspired work and is inspiring, it is first and foremost a collection of writings about the faith of people over several millennia. Respecting this should invite us to draw out lessons about faith. Attempting to make the Bible a history or science text only diminishes its true importance as an inspiring text.

Dealing with
Spiritually Reborn People

I recently received a letter from a reader of a column I write. He's a man in his mid-twenties. The letter was about his relationship with his roommate, with whom he has been a good friend for several years. "[My roommate] has become 'spiritual' in a big way. It took me by surprise, but I was trying not to let it faze me. Before I go on, let me say that I have nothing against spirituality, but when it is communicated in a way that makes me feel inferior, I have a problem. Do you think you could write a column on how to deal with reborn spiritual people?"

The writer's particular situation is not uncommon. Whether a person has the kind of born-again experience common among evangelical Christians or some other type of spiritual awakening, it is often difficult for friends and family members to understand the changes the person experiences at a time of spiritual awakening. This is especially true when those closest to the individual find inconsistencies between the person's behaviors and professed beliefs or when the person seems to have forgotten his or her past or responsibilities after a spiritual awakening.

The writer's response is not unusual in these situations. Attempting to respect the legitimacy of his friend's experience, he tried to just go on with life in a normal way. Obviously, it wasn't working because he began to feel that his friend's newfound life perspective made him feel inferior.

The writer continues, "[My roommate] seems to be finding 'personality' in everyday objects—he has even gone so far as to say that certain things speak to him, so he has to get them. In addition, he is taking whole rolls of film to record everyday objects, like flowers, pots, weight-room plates, the sky, sunsets—you name it! He has described various stories where he is just in awe, like a child is, about everyday occurrences that I guess we overburdened folk take for granted, like cloud formations, sunsets, and trees. I don't know where this is coming from, but I feel that he is finally transforming into the person he probably was always meant to be. I am not disappointed, but I am afraid that we are losing touch with one another."

Authentic spiritual awakenings open us to perceive and apprehend life in new ways. Sometimes that means we get a sense of the big picture of life, a sense of balance and harmony in the cosmos, rather than just seeing our small part of the world. At other times, we realize that it is the ordinary events of life that contain meaning. At such times, we realize that there is beauty and mystery in the natural order, as in the sun rising, a flower blooming, or a bird's flight. We are filled with a sense of awe for these things. We reverence life—its strength, simplicity, and order—in a new way. Those things are very good and a sign that something has changed about the way we perceive the world around us.

In a real way, spirituality opens us more deeply to all life around us. A healthy, balanced spiritual life does not diminish our life perspective. In fact, it should open us further to the mystery of life we consider Sacred in ourselves, the world around us, and other people. There are times, however, when spiritual development requires that we separate ourselves from others for prayer and meditation, retreat, or study.

The writer seems able to identify the valid spiritual experiences his friend is having while also being aware that something about it is not quite right. His fear is the loss of friendship.

It is important to remember that growth in any area of our life is rarely smooth; it is usually awkward. More often than not, we stumble and fall before learning to walk and trip ourselves up in the process of learning to run. Growth in all areas of our life is generally not balanced from the start, but in time can be integrated in a balanced way.

In considering some of that awkward process associated with learning to walk a spiritual path, I'd like to discuss some specific things to consider when someone has a new spiritual awakening that those close to the person don't really understand.

First, a spiritual awakening of any kind presents a person with a larger, broader, or different perspective of life than the person previously had. It takes time to integrate this new perspective with the rest of life. It's important to allow those close to us to have the time they need for this step of personal growth. In other words, the best way to keep a friend is to be a friend. Friendship requires patient understanding.

Second, a radical spiritual awakening often empowers people to make fundamental changes in life. Spiritual awakenings cause people to stop years of alcohol or drug dependency, change manipulative or dishonest behavior, and break harmful patterns of living that have persisted for years. When someone is undergoing this level of change, that person is so zealous that he or she may tax the patience of even the most devout believer. However, these are life-saving changes that should be supported. Again, with patience and proper direction, a person is often able to integrate the changes and lead life in a more relaxed and contented way.

Third, if someone close to you is experiencing some sort of spiritual awakening that is putting stress on your relationship, talk to the person about it in a nonjudgmental way. Tell the person, "I know something new has happened in your life. I don't really understand it. Can you tell me about it?" If the new pursuits are making you feel uncomfortable, talk about that, too. Say something like, "Your friendship is very important to me. Since this change has happened, I'm afraid I might be losing your friendship. Can we talk about it?" Chances are that the person is unaware how the changes are affecting you. That's not because the friend is self-centered but rather that something important occurred that has captured the person's full attention.

Lastly, not all things labeled "spiritual" are healthy or beneficial. Healthy, authentic spiritual growth makes people more open and respectful of others. Unhealthy pseudospirituality creates judgmental, critical people. Watch for patterns over several months. If someone claims to have had a conversion experience that results in them treating others badly, breaking off relationships for seemingly no reason, and becoming irresponsible about commitments, there is cause for alarm. Speak to the person and be specific about the behavior that appears dangerous, saying something like, "When you say I am not enlightened enough to understand, I feel ..." If this kind of discussion is not helpful, speak to a religious or spiritual teacher. Sometimes, what appears to be spiritual enlightenment is a sign of psychological instability or indoctrination into a cult. Someone with more expertise in this area can help sort out what is happening.

More often than not, enthusiasm after a spiritual awakening is a normal, healthy sign of personal growth. Most people simply need the patience and understanding of their friends in the process. Being a good friend during these periods of growth often helps to cement the bonds of friendship.

PART TWO:
LESSONS ON THE RHYTHM IN DAILY LIFE

It's Morning: Stumbling into The Day

It was morning. I stumbled from my bedroom and made my way to the kitchen. I was glad I remembered to set up the coffeepot last night. Automatic timers are a wonderful invention. After pouring a cup of freshly brewed coffee, I headed to the balcony. From my balcony seat, I looked out over Biscayne Bay. I took a deep breath and began to sip my first cup of morning coffee. Yes, it was good.

Biscayne Bay: this body of water between Miami and Miami Beach had been a source of solitude and solace for me during my years living in South Florida. Living on a small island in the middle of the bay, I had grown used to the breeze coming off the water, the sound of waves, reflections of sunlight, blue skies, myriad cloud formations, and the flight path of a wide variety of birds.

Morning is a special time on the bay. Pelicans and gulls glide over the bay with ease. Occasional egrets, most often found inland, sometimes venture this way, too. From their airborne travels, my winged friends would suddenly dive into the blue crystal water, returning to flight with the catch of the day.

Winter mornings welcomed the dolphins at play, bouncing along the waves. Never alone, but traveling in pods, their bodies arched up along the waves, bouncing with the wave patterns. Watching them, I would smile and remember a verse of Psalm 104 about Leviathan, the great fish God made for Divine amusement.

In both winter and summer, other companions were always waiting for me. Surprisingly, the ones who taught me the most as I watched from my balcony perch were the wise old buzzards. These carnivorous winged creatures seemed frightful when I watched them tear apart a fresh carcass; yet this macabre image was transformed in flight. Buzzards glide effortlessly on the breezes, climbing higher than any other bird in this environment. In groups of three or four, their circular flight paths cross and intersect almost in a spiral dance. Gliding onto an upward wind vent, they climb higher and higher, then spin off to soar, gazing down on the distant land and water in seemingly effortless flight. No struggle or work. Simply gliding on the current and allowing them to be taken where they need to be. The buzzards teach a lesson about the mysterious balance of pain and beauty in life.

It is with this community of winged creatures and fish that I began each day with a time of prayer and meditation. It was from this perch that I learned lessons about life, its richness and fullness, and the deep wisdom to be learned from our environment.

I left my home on an island in Biscayne Bay. Leaving behind a lush rich environment of tropical life, I ventured to Arizona in hopes of responding to a different sense of call. Responding to this call has led me to the desert, the spiritual place of preparation.

The intense dryness and heat of the desert causes one to examine life in particular ways. What is really needed for survival? How does one function in the heat of each day? How can I best pace myself for the long haul through the heat? These day-to-day questions of desert dwellers, which cause one to make sure to travel with water and newcomers like myself to acquire a taste for sport beverages, are important spiritual questions for our lives. What is really necessary for our lives? How do we make it when the heat of life challenges us in fundamental ways? How do we pace the rhythm of our lives for the long haul when conflicting values and responsibilities pull us in myriad directions?

The only resolutions I find for the reality of life's challenges and questions come from the rhythm of prayer. While we often look for quick answers, finding ways to lead a graceful life comes from patience and persistence. Answers don't come magically. The resolutions to the challenges of life slowly grow from within us.

So it is that in the morning, I stumble from my bedroom and make my way to the kitchen. I'm glad I remembered to set up the coffeepot the night before. Automatic timers are a wonderful invention. After pouring a cup of freshly brewed coffee, I now head to other places to pray. From morning walks in a desert Zen garden, I learn what it means to put down roots in dry, sandy soil and soak in the moisture that continues to give life during many hot days. Yes, there is deep wisdom to be learned from our environment.

The Rhythm of Morning

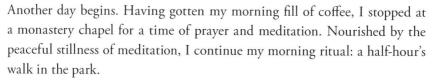

Another day begins. Having gotten my morning fill of coffee, I stopped at a monastery chapel for a time of prayer and meditation. Nourished by the peaceful stillness of meditation, I continue my morning ritual: a half-hour's walk in the park.

It's September. Now that school is back in session, the park has returned to its familiar tranquility. Over the summer months, there was an activities program for kids in the park. Each morning, the young people gathered for things like softball and soccer. With school back to its normal schedule, it's just me and a couple of dogs who make sure that their owners are properly exercised.

It's just after 8:00 a.m. as the last of the sprinklers turn off, leaving the grass moist and fresh. As I walk several laps around the park, my steps form a pace that continues to balance and settle me. This morning time is invigorating for me.

Yes, this time in the morning is important to me. The rhythm of prayer and exercise helps attune me to the spirit of life within and around me. The balance of both activities fosters within me an awareness of the rich wholeness that forms the magical fabric of life.

Sometimes my walk gives me time to focus on specific projects I have that day. It's occasionally during these walks that I mentally outline articles like these, sort out how best to work with a client, or organize my thoughts for a class that I'm teaching. Those aren't bad things to do on my morning walk. But the real gift of my time walking occurs when I'm not using the time for planning. The real gift of walking each morning comes when I'm present to life in the park.

This morning, the ground is soft under my feet from the hard rain of last night. The air is especially sweet. Perhaps the rain has brought fresh blooms to a plant with which I'm not familiar. But today, it's mostly the birds and butterflies that have my attention.

Several small orange-yellow desert butterflies flutter close to the ground. I suspect that they like this park because it's one of the few places for them to find wide-open grass. This morning they seem to dance to a silent song, making circular flights of fancy, stopping to rest occasionally on taller blades of grass. If I could only be so carefree and not take life so seriously! They remind me to trust the cycle of life and nature that orders the lives of all creatures.

The birds seem to have extra energy this morning. They fly in small flocks, landing for a brief time in one spot and then flitting off to the next. A dog runs into their midst, and they fly off for the safety of a tree. As they pick at the ground looking for food and sip water from the puddles along the walking trail, I am reminded of their basic trust in life: yes, everything that is needed has been provided. The birds of the air remind me of those simple lessons.

The best mornings in the park are when I simply allow myself to be in tune with the wonder of nature around me. There are many lessons to be learned from the simple winged and four-legged creatures that make this place their home. Perhaps most important are the gentle reminders to slow down and stay in tune with the cycle of life. It's so easy to get caught up in the frantic pace and find one's spirit slipping away. Taking time each day for my morning ritual of meditation and walking helps to keep me balanced and give me the focus I need for the day.

It's not long before my walk in the park comes to an end. It's time to get home and shower before heading to the office for an appointment. Back in my car, I turn onto a major street and am jarred by the rush of traffic. Yes, school is back in session. It seems as though overnight the number of cars at this hour has doubled.

As cars weave from one lane to another, with a slow car in the fast lane and a fast car trying to push ahead in the slow lane, we're all stopped a few yards ahead by a changing light. I'm glad that I'm able to take the balance of my morning time with me. I smile to myself and wonder: What would this busy morning traffic be like if more people took time each day to be focused and centered? How would all of our lives be different if more people incorporated contemplative practices into their daily lives? Perhaps it's best not to focus on others and to simply be mindful of one's own spiritual path and appreciate the beauty of each moment.

A Time for Quiet

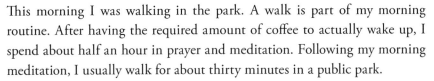

This morning I was walking in the park. A walk is part of my morning routine. After having the required amount of coffee to actually wake up, I spend about half an hour in prayer and meditation. Following my morning meditation, I usually walk for about thirty minutes in a public park.

Today, as I walked, my mind wandered to a conversation with friends this past weekend. I was in Los Angeles. The trip allowed me to spend time with two long-standing friends, a psychiatrist and a psychologist. As we talked about our work, I heard how my psychiatrist friend went early each morning to the hospital to see patients; from there to his private practice office; and then to the training institute where he also worked. It sounded like more than a full day to me. My psychologist friend had just returned from lecturing in six cities in ten days. He spends much of his time on the road while working with clients by telephone. I wondered if they had much time to be quiet and still on any regular basis.

As I walked, I also thought about the last client I saw yesterday. She is a bright, energetic professional woman. She administers the day-to-day operations of a large nonprofit agency, she is involved in community groups, and she's raising a child with her partner. She came to see me because of insomnia, stress, and stomach irritation. While her physician prescribed medication for these symptoms, it didn't really solve the problem. I've been working with my client to slow down, relax, and allow herself to experience her emotions rather than keep things bottled inside while spending her waking hours "in charge" of everything. It's been a struggle for her to slow down and allow her mind to become quiet and still.

Many people today struggle with the amount of work they face, the demands on their time, and the pace of managing task after task. Sometimes this hectic pace is associated with a high salary level. Often, it is not. No matter what the financial benefits of such a lifestyle, it inevitably pulls us away from ourselves and prevents us from being "at home" with who we are most deeply.

A vital spiritual practice and an important aspect of personal growth is taking time for self each day to simply be still. Often, creating that space is like trying to push a lot of water uphill. The demands on our time keep pressing down and prevent us from having the quality time we need.

By taking time to be quiet each day, we begin to let go of the demands and expectations placed on us by others (and often the expectations we place on ourselves). In their place, our emotions and feelings about our lives begin to surface. As we sort out our emotions, both the joys and the concerns, we have the opportunity to simply rest with the person we are most deeply. That quiet rest gives us the opportunity to restore our energy and be renewed with a different kind of clarity on life. When time in quiet becomes a regular part of our lives, we are less likely to be jostled back and forth by the demands of our lives, and we walk through life with a greater sense of calm and assurance.

Whether it is in the form of meditation or the time to walk the dog, each of us needs to break away from the concerns of everyday life long enough to permit everything to go quiet inside us. The process of letting everything go quiet inside is the process of returning to the center of who we are. It is when we learn to live from the center of who we are that we can engage in our work and relationships with freedom and spontaneity.

Taking time for quiet each day: it's a very simple practice. Yet, in its simplicity, it can enable us to experience much greater depth in life.

Living Life the Way It Should Be

It was a little after ten in the morning. The sun was already hot. The air was thick and humid. It took effort to walk at a pace faster than a stroll. Coming from the Sonoran Desert, I had forgotten what the heat and humidity of South Florida were like. The air was thick and heavy.

I walked the boardwalk slowly. Around me cypress trees created the frame for the hammock made of dense vegetation. I moved out of the sun and walked deeper into the Everglades. Little lizards, mostly brown, sometimes fluorescent green, would scurry away from my path. I paused to watch an alligator as she rested her snout on a log, dozing, keeping cool in the water.

I had driven this Saturday morning from Miami Beach to the interior of Florida. My destination was the Seminole reservation. I knew it would be quiet in the cypress wetlands of the Everglades. I spent a few hours in the calm stillness of the Glades, staying mostly on the boardwalk and out of the murky waters.

Contrary to popular belief, the Everglades is not a swamp. It's actually a broad, slow-moving river of grassy water. Like the Sonoran Desert, it is one of the most delicate habitats on this continent. Also like the Sonoran Desert, it is threatened by ever-expanding development and the far-from-subtle human presence.

During this visit to the Glades, I watched alligators, turtles, fish, birds, lizards, snakes, and winged and four-legged creatures of many varieties. I examined trees, vines, bushes, ferns, and other vegetation of rich greens and deep browns. I could not help but be overwhelmed with the balance and harmony found in this remote place.

Staying for a time on the edge of the water, I could sense the southward movement of the water. Could I see it? Was I intuiting it? I really don't know. Yet I found that I moved out of myself and into a level of communion with this environment. The stillness, balance, and harmony of this place became part of me for a brief while.

It was clear that the natural inhabitants of this place live in a wisdom that we two-legged creatures often miss. They possess the ability to simply be and live peacefully in their home. The gentle flow of the water, the heat of the sun, and the humidity of the air are not struggled against but accepted and lived with. Our four-legged and winged relatives live in the flow of life around them and move with it, not against it.

Within thirty minutes' drive of this calm place, I was back to a different order of life. Humans rushed on the freeway, cutting each other off to get ahead of each other. People were in their own worlds in cars and homes and offices pursuing tasks to which they'd given great importance. The calm of the day for many people would be reduced to an evening cocktail, a hit of some drug, or an emotional release aimed at harming another. Our lives have strayed so far from the simple balance that is part of the fabric of life as it was created.

Many days I wonder if we humans will simply spin ourselves out of control. In some ways, perhaps we already have. Yet no matter what stress and confusion I experience living life as a human being, I find solace in knowing that in the heart of the Everglades, there's an alligator resting her snout on a log, dozing, and keeping cool in the water, living life the way it should be.

Slowing Down and
Taking Time for Ourselves

Slowing down and taking time for oneself is usually more difficult for people than it sounds. First, there's the problem of making time in our lives for ourselves. But once we've done that, what do we do with the time?

I was recently visiting Washington DC and stayed with a good friend of mine, Bill. Bill is a talented, articulate, professional guy in his thirties. He recently left a position with a corporate consulting firm, where he traveled a great deal for work and put in long hours. As we visited in his living room Saturday morning, he told me a bit about his new job. "I think the most difficult part of the new job," he said, jesting, "is that I'm really done at five o'clock! I can't remember when I was able to leave work on time and only put in forty hours a week. I have so much time on my hands, I'm not sure what to do with it all."

In truth, I know that Bill is putting that time to good use. He's working on a few improvements on his home. The weekend I was there, he planned a party with his friends. "It's great to have time to invite people over. I haven't been able to do that much," Bill told me as he showed me the invitation he created on his computer.

Many people have difficulty filling spare time once they have it. It's often easy to fill it with busy activities or to find ways of creating more work for oneself. There's also the solution of filling time by hanging out for endless hours online, talking about not much of anything in chat rooms or endlessly surfing the web.

It's my experience that many people find themselves bored when faced with free, unstructured time. Few of us have learned how to engage ourselves in ways other than work or spectator entertainment. If there's not work to be done or entertainment to occupy us, what are we going to do?

Healthy, integrated personal and spiritual growth requires that we learn to quiet ourselves inside and learn to be still. Learning to quiet the heart and mind does not come naturally to us. We've learned to be thinking people, using our minds to stay tuned to what's happening around us. Our emotional connections to people and activities draw us out of ourselves. When thoughts or emotional contact is gone, what is left?

Being quiet and still inside allows us to experience life in a different, very subtle way. It is through inner quiet that we are able to let go of the excess baggage that clutters our lives, explore creative endeavors, and bring a different shape or context to our lives. But the quiet and stillness startle us or sometimes make us fearful at first. We can't tell if there's anything there at all. Or worse, perhaps it seems like the only thing inside is pain.

The practice of slowing down, allowing ourselves to be quiet inside, opens us to a depth of inner life that is both healing and renewing for us. As with anything new, we sometimes find inner quiet uncomfortable or unfamiliar. But with time, what starts as uncomfortable can become a good habit that makes us richer, fuller people.

The first step toward inner quiet is simply taking the time. Bill was lucky: his job change unexpectedly gave him more space in his life. Many of us need to go the harder route and consciously claim free space for ourselves in our busy days.

Dreams and Waking Reality:
A Reflection

I sat in a circle with a group of about a dozen other people. We completed a guided meditation and quietly paged through copies of several poems provided by the group's leader. Each person quietly read aloud one of the poems, reflecting on lines or stanzas that stirred some meaning or resonance.

I found myself drawn to this line from R. Tagore's "Crossing":

> REJOICE!
> For Night's fetters have broken, the
>   dreams have vanished.
> Thy word has rent its veils, the buds of
>   morning are opened; awake O sleeper!
> Light's greetings spread from the East
>   to the West,
> And at the ramparts of the ruined prison
>   rise the paeans of Victory!*

While I'm not familiar with the body of Tagore's work, I am aware that he is a noted Bengali poet who won the Nobel Prize for Literature in 1913. Hearing this poem read in this reflective group experience, the first line of this stanza struck me: "REJOICE! For Night's fetters have broken, the dreams have vanished."

---

* *Rabindranath Tagore, Lover's Gift and Crossing,* published by MacMillan Company in 1918; now in public domain.

I thought about how often I have encouraged others (and have been encouraged by others) to follow dreams. Each of us has dreams for our future, hopes for things to come, and visions of what we long will come to pass. Some of those dreams and visions are projections of our desires. Others, I believe, are inspirations we receive. In either case, I believe it is important to pay attention to our dreams and visions for the future, to understand them, and to wisely consider how they draw us toward (or away from) the options life presents to us.

Following dreams and visions is tricky business. We always need to consider the ramifications of our actions. Is a dream practical, healthy for us, and respectful of others? Sometimes we find that a dream or vision is so strong and draws us so intensely that we seem to have no other option than to throw caution to the wind and make a leap of faith into an unknown future. We hope that the dream will sustain us and that all will be well because of our faith. But there are no guarantees that we will be right (or wrong) in our course of action. Only time will tell.

What will time demonstrate about our dreams? Tagore says it poetically: Night's fetters will be broken, and dreams will vanish in the light of day. Following our dreams will lead us somewhere. But where? Often it is surprising where we find ourselves. My experience tells me that in the light of day, when I can see the place where my dreams have led me, I'm not exactly where I thought I would end up. That's not necessarily bad.

To make this concrete, let me share from my own experience. After my employer in Miami unexpectedly ceased operation due to financial difficulties, I moved in 1997 from Miami to Tucson. Something inside convinced me that Tucson was the right place for me. There were some words of encouragement from others and several promises of things that would happen by moving to Arizona. I settled in Tucson, mostly enjoying the life I've made for myself. I followed the dream and paid close attention to the vision. In the move, I risked a great deal. My life bore little resemblance to the life I thought I would lead there. For instance, a job offer in Arizona made to me before I moved did not work out. I had some scrambling to do because of it. Then, as life unfolded, I found I really was where I am supposed to be. It's not what I expected, but it's proven to be very good.

Had I clung too tightly to the dreams and vision, the daylight would have dispelled the night and I would have been disappointed. Instead, I was able to look again and see that, while dreams and vision led me, other things have sustained me for the long haul.

My experience is not unique. In many ways, each of us feels drawn into the future by dreams and visions. Our movement forward into the future depends on our willingness to explore those dreams and, at times, make the leap of faith. No matter what the dream, the daylight comes and we discover that it was only a dream. Dreams bring us forward to new places, where the goodness of life can be embraced and celebrated in unique and different ways. So dare to dream. But appreciate the life circumstances that are the places your dreams lead you.

IN THE STILLNESS OF THE NIGHT

We had just finished dinner. The food was great, but the conversation and companionship were even better. The four of us got into my car and started to drive away from the restaurant. It was around 9:30 p.m.

"How would you like to watch the stars for a little while?" I asked my companions. "There's a full moon, and it's a great night." We all agreed to watch the evening sky, so I made the turn onto the Catalina Highway, driving up a mountainside on the outskirts of town.

I was entertaining friends of mine from Washington DC. They were spending a few days in Tucson on vacation before heading off to San Francisco. They decided that they wanted to spend time in the desert and exchange rings as a symbol of their commitment after two years together. Knowing that this was the romantic part of their trip, I thought it would be great to go to one of the overlooks and allow them some time to enjoy the evening.

As we drove up into the foothills and entered the Coronado National Forest, my guests commented about the sharp curves and rocky cliffs. That was all the encouragement I needed to drive a little faster. Having grown up in the mountains, I enjoy driving steep roads.

It wasn't long before we reached the overlook. We parked the car among a few others. We giggled as we passed a teenage couple in the backseat of a car. "Should I ask them for directions to a gas station?" I jokingly asked my friends. With big grins and hopes that the young lovers were being safe, we walked along the retaining wall and began to take in the amazing view.

I jumped up on the wall and perched on the granite surface with my legs dangling off the side. As I looked up, a shooting star darted across the sky. Below us the lights of Tucson spread through the valley. A bank of thick clouds rolled in over the moon. Perhaps it would rain later that night as the last remnant of the monsoon season.

We all became very quiet as we watched the stars and clouds. The thick clouds cast an eerie glow in the sky. The stars twinkled as we silently watched, each looking for familiar constellations or other patterns. Sounds of insects and wildlife in the distance were the only things to break the silence.

At times like this, life takes on a different perspective for me. Surrounded by the vast expanse of nature, I discover a great sense of calm and strength. It's clear how small my day-to-day concerns really are. Surrounded by mountains that have stood for thousands of years, watching stars and planets whose life and vastness are greater than anything I can conceive, sensing the rhythms of the passage of time, I am overwhelmed by both the beautiful simplicity and amazing complexity of life.

That night, as I sat in the stillness of the night with good friends close by, I remembered the words of one of the great mystical writers of the Christian tradition: Julian of Norwich. Living in England during the time of the plague, suffering from a fever that almost took her life, Julian had a wonderful vision. She later wrote about the vision:

> *[God] showed me a little thing, the quantity of a hazelnut, in the palm of my hand; and it was as round as a ball. I looked upon it with eye of my understanding, and thought: What may this be? And I was answered generally thus: It is all that is made. I marveled how it might last, for I thought it might suddenly have fallen to naught for its littleness. And I was answered in my understanding: It lasts, and ever shall last because God loves it. And so all-thing have being by the love of God.**

Indeed, all the wonder of our cosmos, both fragile and powerful, came to be out of a divine affection. Life itself continues out of this same love. How difficult it is for us with our daily concerns to savor and appreciate the

---

*   Julian of Norwich, adapted from *Revelations of Divine Love*, translated by Grace Warrack. First published in 1901, it is now in public domain and available from Christian Classics Ethereal Library at http://www.ccel.org/ccel/julian/revelations.all.html.

care that is the foundation of the universe. But sometimes in the stillness of a desert night, sitting with friends looking at stars and watching the patterns of clouds roll past, we have an opportunity to look again and see that all life is sustained out of love.

PART THREE:
LESSONS ON EMOTIONAL WELL-BEING

FEELINGS, NOTHING MORE THAN FEELINGS

What is it about feelings? Did you ever notice how they have a way of getting us into trouble? We get angry. We yell or do something extreme to express the anger. Afterward, we have to apologize. Or perhaps we get angry, and because we don't want to hurt anyone or look foolish to others, we do what we can to suppress the anger. But in time, we feel the effects of suppressing the anger, and that results in stress.

Love—now that's a feeling that causes trouble. You fall in love, and those feelings get started and everything seems to be turned upside down. You want to tell someone that you love him or her. The tension in doing that! What if they don't feel the same way? Oh, no! The person just said they don't feel the same way. More feelings! Embarrassment! Rejection! What do I do now?

Feelings! What good are they? Mr. Spock in the original *Star Trek* knew they were illogical. Then, in *Star Trek: Next Generation*, Mr. Data, the android, did everything he could to develop feelings. Isn't that the way we are? When we have the feelings, we don't want them. But when we can't have them, nothing becomes more important.

Feelings, or more correctly emotions, are very confusing for most people. We all have them. But few of us know how to use them well.

Over the last thirty years or so, psychologists have been telling people to express their feelings. In the sixties, we let it all hang out. In the seventies, we let it out with a primal scream. In the eighties, we paid attention to others' feelings. In the nineties, we learned that what we did in the eighties was codependent. We learned to guard our boundaries so as to not let others disrupt our personal space and comfort zone. Now, it's the second decade of the first century of the third millennium! Is there a chance that we can understand our emotions in a way that works?

Emotions, after all, are a biological reality. They are caused when neurochemical substances are released by our brains and swim around in our bodies. When we experience emotions, there are both physiological and psychological dimensions to our experience. We feel both physiologically and psychologically. That's how we are made.

Emotions are part of our makeup. Not only is that true for humans, but it's true for dogs, cats, and other mammals. The brains of mammals produce chemicals that result in the feelings known as emotions. Unlike many other mammals, humans possess an upper level of brain development that allows us to reason and make choices.

Culturally, we've been taught that anything painful or uncomfortable is bad and should be stopped. Our feelings sometimes make us feel bad and often make us uncomfortable. So, we do what we can to stop them. We try to cut them off by our own willpower. When that doesn't work, we use drugs, alcohol, food, or anything else to either dull the pain or create an escape from the feeling. That works for a while. For example, a shy person goes to a bar to meet someone. The shy person has a few drinks and no longer feels "shy." Since the alcohol killed the emotional sensation of shyness, the person is much freer to meet someone. It works. But there are several downsides to this solution. The shy person may have to drink so much to deaden those feelings that the shy person ends up a sloppy drunk. If the shy person uses this as a solution long enough, dependency develops. Over more time, the shy person becomes an addict and is focused more on drinking. Meeting people becomes irrelevant.

Wouldn't it be easier just to learn about emotions? Rather than avoid emotions because they are either painful or unpleasant, since we have to have them, doesn't it make sense to learn to use them? Of course it does! But that takes time and some work. Most of us opt for the easier solution of avoidance rather than learning to use our emotions as the important ally they are.

It seems to me that most people fall into one of two categories when it comes to emotions. Most people avoid their feelings. Actually, our society supports the notion of anesthetizing emotions. Many people have learned not to let anything "get to them." So, they usually find a way to do that. If they can't repress their feelings themselves, they use a substance or compulsive behavior to numb the emotions. Then there are the people at the other end of the spectrum. They seem to wear their hearts on their sleeves. When they have any kind of emotion, they pay close attention to it and make their decisions based on it. Both extremes cause people lots of difficulties in life, relationships, and self-perception.

As with most things in life, there is a middle ground when it comes to emotions. It is challenging to learn to live life from that emotional middle ground. However, life from this balanced perspective can be very rich indeed.

Emotions are part of our experience. They are biologically based. We experience an emotion because a chemical has been released in our brain and is having an effect on our body. The chemical is automatically released. Since emotional responses are part of the standard equipment of our bodies, it makes sense to make good use of them.

Beginning to learn to make good use of our feelings is easier than you may suspect. First, because emotions are biological, learning about our feelings means learning about our bodies. Pay attention to what is happening in your body when you experience an emotion. Is your chest or stomach tight? Does your heart feel light? Does your jaw get tense? What change occurs in your body when you experience a particular emotion? When you know this, you'll be able to reverse the observation. I know that when someone is trying to con me in some way, I get a particular feeling in my gut. Sometimes, when I'm working and focused on something and not paying attention to my emotional state, I'll experience that particular feeling in my gut. When I become aware of it, I can ask myself, "What's going on to cause that?" Sure enough, I'll realize that someone is attempting to manipulate and con me in some way.

Among the many things feelings do is provide us with information about what's happening around us. When we understand and use our emotions properly, they are like a barometer measuring what's happening in a particular situation, relationship, or period in our life. Feelings give us signals or clues about everything that's happening in our life. If we're smart, we pay attention to our feelings and learn how to use them.

But what about the emotions that are difficult for us, like sadness, loneliness, or some other kind of pain? They just hurt, don't they? No, not exactly. While it's true that emotional experiences are not always pleasurable, the emotions that don't feel positive to us provide us with very important information about what we need to do. It's important to learn from them. It's also very important to remember that feelings don't last. No matter what the feeling, it's temporary. In a little time, the chemicals the brain releases get reabsorbed in the body, and the feeling is over. However, if we don't pay attention to our feelings, the brain will pump more of the chemicals into our system, and the feeling will keep on going and going for a lot longer. In other words, it hurts because it's trying to get our attention. If all we do is avoid it, our brain tries harder to get our attention. By not paying attention to the sensations, we are merely hurting ourselves.

In 1995, Daniel Goleman wrote the book *Emotional Intelligence*. It's a book I often recommend to people who want to learn more about emotions. In it, he explains how to pay attention to and understand emotions so that you can use them in a smart way. Another book, *Raising Your Emotional Intelligence* by Jeanne Segal, is a collection of easy-to-use lessons to help you use your emotions in the way they were designed. I can't recommend it highly enough.

Feelings. Yes, they're nothing more than feelings. But they can be a great help to us if we use them properly. They are an ally for our strength, well-being, and wholeness.

There are many people who fear or have an apprehension of their feelings. Strong emotions can be overwhelming. They leave us with a sense of being out of control. Rather than being overwhelmed by the intensity of our emotions or fearing that we'd do something we really don't want to do if our feelings get loose, most people keep their feelings tightly locked inside. My best recommendation for those in this kind of a situation is to find a good counselor to help sort out the feelings that have been buried deep inside.

Many people don't seek counseling because they are afraid of the pain they'll have to face or because counseling could mean dredging up things they'd rather forget. However, there are three forms of therapy commonly practiced in Tucson that make dealing with strong emotions much easier than most people would expect. Those therapies are EMDR, thought-field therapy, and hypnosis. Let me explain a little about each of them.

EMDR stands for Eye Movement Desensitization and Reprocessing. This is a simple form of therapy where someone thinks about a difficult memory. The therapist directs the client in a series of eye movements using a light machine. This therapy causes the person to imitate the eye movements of deep sleep. Through this process, the memory is integrated in a new way and the difficult emotions are released. Studies demonstrate that this form of therapy is highly successful, especially with traumatic memories.

Thought-field therapy uses a different approach. People are taught to do a series of body tapping gestures when they experience fear or anxiety; the tapping stimulates the release of biochemicals, which result in decrease of the anxiety or fear.

While I know about these two forms of treatment, they are not techniques I use. My preference as a clinician is hypnotherapy. The reason I like hypnotherapy over other forms of treatment is because it is so versatile. It can be used for everything from overcoming traumatic memories and releasing fears and phobias, to improving memory and athletic performance.

In hypnosis, the body is usually very relaxed, while the brain remains active using alpha and theta brain-wave patterns. These brain waves are the same as those we experience in deep relaxation, sleep, and dreaming. Only in hypnosis, we are awake. In this state, we can remember past events or imagine future possibilities as though they were present time. From that vantage point, we can release pain, anger, or other hurts that only limit us. Or we can incorporate new behaviors and attitudes.

With hypnosis, as with any form of therapy, it's important to be sure that the counselor or therapist is properly trained and experienced. I've worked with many clients who were harmed by hypnotherapists (and other kinds of therapists) who really didn't know what they were doing and made things worse rather than better. When looking for a therapist of any type, be sure to ask direct questions about the therapist's training, experience, and certifications. If the counselor is vague about her or his training and experience or becomes annoyed by such questions, it's a sign that the therapist may not be the right one for you.

In sum, emotions are an important part of how we are made. They aren't just about how we feel, but are about our biology and our attitude and outlook on life. Learn to use your emotions as the important resources they are. If that means working with a counselor to help you take full advantage of the strength emotions can be, go for it! The benefit will be greater than you can imagine.

It Makes Me Nervous

She's a bright articulate woman in her early forties. Following her divorce, her husband gained custody of their children. A few years ago, she moved to Tucson to start a new life working in the high-tech industry. Now living with a new partner, she is working through many past hurts and is trying to understand the role spirituality has in her life.

As we talked, she told me about her recovery from early childhood sexual abuse. She realized that the abusive pattern she learned in childhood was repeated with her husband. She understands how difficult it is for her to trust anyone else in a relationship.

Her story is not unusual. Actually, it's more common than any of us want to think. Her experience is not common only among women. Many gay men could tell very similar stories about their past.

The process of integrating a sense of wholeness and well-being when childhood was shattered by sexual, physical, or emotional abuse is challenging for anyone. Our early childhood experiences teach us how to relate to other people, both for good and for ill. That's why survivors find themselves repeating the patterns of abuse over again in other relationships. Yet the human spirit is resilient. Well-being can be restored. While I don't believe we are ever "as good as new" (because we cannot change the past), we can reestablish a sense of wholeness and balance in our lives. Learning how to trust others and doing so wisely is an important part of that process.

As significant as the work this woman had completed was for her healing, she told me again and again something that a spiritual teacher taught her. That's what made me nervous. The woman explained that she knew the reason she could develop a spiritual life was because of the sexual abuse she suffered. The spiritual teacher convinced her that it was the abuse that opened her to spirituality and for that she should be thankful.

While I am very clear in my own beliefs, I have learned to be very respectful of the beliefs of others. There are times, however, when beliefs that have been imposed on others are very dangerous to their well-being. When I speak with other people and it appears that some of their beliefs may be dangerous to their well-being, I do what I can to empower them to explore beliefs that may be healthier for them.

It is very important that survivors of early childhood trauma understand that nothing they did caused the abuse and that they are in no way responsible for it. Sexual, physical, and emotional abuse is wrong. Perpetrators often have a history of abuse in their own lives. That doesn't make abuse less wrong. It simply demonstrates that the evil of child abuse passes from generation to generation. Are abusers evil people? No. But abusive actions and behavior may well be viewed as bad or evil.

The wonder of the human spirit is that even in the midst of very bad circumstances, we still have the ability to grow and be more than our limited circumstances seem to allow. In terms of spiritual growth, even in the midst of great pain we are able to find goodness, truth, and beauty in life. But spiritual development does not require that one experience horrible suffering in life. Abuse of a person in childhood is not a requirement for the person to be open to the spiritual dimension of life. When someone holds the belief that the childhood abuse that was part of the person's life was a necessary condition for spiritual growth, that person is never able to recover from the abuse. This kind of belief enshrines the abuse in a person's life rather than letting go of the pain to move on for the sake of recovery. Holding onto past abuse can result in a crippling condition for one's psychological and spiritual health. It is a way of reinforcing the abuse rather than facilitating healing.

Survivors of childhood sexual abuse often find that spiritual development is a vital part of their recovery, and so they take it very seriously. That's a very important distinction. Having survived serious abuse, one may develop the capacity to be more empathetic toward others. But that's a result of the healing, not a result of the abuse itself.

Yes, I get very nervous when ill-trained spiritual teachers or religious leaders perpetuate cycles of abuse by convincing their devotees that horrible experiences of life are to be thankfully embraced for their own good. It's unfortunate that little can be done to stop such teachers and preachers. However, concerned friends and loved ones can offer positive support and suggest that those working toward healing from abuse use sound judgment and common sense.

INTEGRITY AND AUTHENTICITY: FACING LIFE CHALLENGES

This morning, I met with a client. She's a woman I enjoy working with. While we're technically using hypnosis to help her with weight loss, we also talk a great deal about her spiritual life. Because of the depth of her spirituality, I enjoy these conversations.

At the end of our session today, she told me a story on which she frequently reflects. It is a story about a Buddhist monastery in the mountains of Tibet. The events occurred in the early years of the Chinese occupation of Tibet. For generations, the monastery had thrived in its remote location. Many people there thought they were safe from the foreign invaders. But in time, word came to the monks and the people of the town that the Chinese were heading their way. Knowing of the destruction of other monasteries and the thousands of monks who had been killed, the monks decided that they would flee the monastery to hide in the mountains. Perhaps, they thought, fewer monks and townspeople would be killed and the town would be safer. So, all the monks left the monastery and went into hiding, except one older monk who insisted on staying behind.

Shortly after the monks left the monastery, the Chinese army arrived. The townspeople told the Chinese commander that all the monks had fled to the mountains, except one old monk who closed himself in the monastery. The commander was infuriated. Not only did he want the monks captured, but he was outraged that this older monk dared to remain behind, as though one old monk could save the fate of the monastery. The commander took some members of his forces and broke down the monastery door. Inside the courtyard, he found the monk seated in meditation. Drawing his sword, the commander took a firm stance in front of the monk, who remained unmoved. "Do you not know who I am?" asked the commander. "I am the one who can thrust this sword through your heart!" Calmly, and with great dignity, the monk looked the commander in the eye and responded, "Do you not know who I am? I am the one who can allow you to thrust your sword through my heart."

My training as a psychologist has taught me the importance for individuals to set appropriate boundaries for themselves, to care for themselves by taking responsibility for their own needs in life, and to remove themselves from abusive, harmful situations. Strong ego development is good psychology. But human growth is more than just ego development.

There are times in life when our spiritual beliefs and values cause us to make difficult choices. To make these choices requires that we have sufficient knowledge of ourselves. It is when we know who we are and can stand firmly in that knowledge (what psychology calls ego strength and self-esteem) that we can truly live according to our beliefs. Sometimes, living according to our beliefs and spiritual values causes us pain. While some people think that spirituality is a matter of experiencing peace and contentment, in fact, authentic spiritual development is not an escape from the real world. The real world includes pain and suffering. Spirituality empowers us to be open to find deeper meaning in life as it comes our way and challenges us to live with integrity to the stirrings deep within us. This kind of spirituality sometimes requires that we embrace pain and hardship in life for some greater benefit. Suffering is not admirable for its own sake. However, living with authenticity and integrity can cause us pain.

While the story of the monastery has no further ending, we know that many Tibetan Buddhist monks did not flee the Chinese takeover and faced death bravely. As a group, they were not helpless victims of oppression. Rather, because their beliefs empowered them to continue to live with integrity, many of these monks freely accepted their fate, looking at it head-on with eyes wide-open. They knew who they were, stood true to their values, and remained faithful to what was true for them, even in the face of death. Few of us will face such drastic life events as a foreign invasion. Yet we each experience challenges to our values and beliefs. Authentic spiritual growth enables us to

Sounds and Silence

In addition to my work as a therapist and spiritual director, I teach at one of the local universities in the area of counseling psychology. This week, I read a stack of student papers on the topic of personality. Most of the papers were ordinary. They discussed personality traits and constructs. One paper was more personal than most of the others. The writer was exploring how his life experience shaped his personality.

This student was born and lived in another country until he was seventeen years of age. At that time, war erupted in his homeland. His family arranged to have him move to the United States. He came here alone, while the rest of his family remained in his native land. The revolution is long over, and a government contrary to his family's politics is now in power. His family suffered a great deal because of the revolution. In the paper, he wrote that he tries not to think about the home and family he left behind, but instead focuses on continuing his life and building a future.

He realized that the one thing that got him through the transition, loss, and intense homesickness was television. He explained in the paper that after arriving in the United States, he began to fill his time by watching TV. It helped him learn American English, customs, and cultural values. It also provided him companionship. While the transition to the United States is many years behind him, he continues to turn on the TV as soon as he walks into his home. It remains on whether he watches it or not. My student explained in the paper that the background noise of the TV prevents him from remembering all that he lost. The TV fills his head with noise so that he doesn't have to hear himself think. Thinking is too painful for him.

While the life experience of this student, who moved to another country for safety in the midst of revolution in his native land, is something with which few of us can identify, part of his story is very familiar. Many people fill their lives with the background noises of TV or music. Often, the background sounds help to fill in the gaps between our activities so that we don't feel alone, disconnected from others, or as in the case of the student, haunted by memories of the past. The experience of silence is very difficult for many people. That's because when we are silent, there is nothing to prevent us from encountering our thoughts, feelings, or memories. In silence, we are left alone with ourselves.

Of course, I enjoy music and have my favorite television programs. Further, there are times when it's good for each of us to get caught up in "mindless" activities to help relieve stress or tension and just relax. At the same time, when we are unable to be comfortably alone and silent, that's a signal that something is out of balance in our lives.

We can presume that my student has many past traumatic events from the revolution and loss of family and homeland that remain difficult for him to deal with. But only he knows what he faces in his thoughts and memories, or what he wants to avoid. Most of us find difficulty facing the ordinary anxieties of life. We wonder whether we are lovable. We hope others won't discover our secret thoughts. We believe that if others knew about something in our past, they would reject us. In silence, the ordinary anxieties of human life begin to slowly come to our awareness. They seem to take hold of us and threaten to have us face things we'd rather avoid.

In the end, we have a choice: we can either dispel these demons from our inner world by facing them, or we can avoid them by filling our lives with noise and activity. It's clear that most people choose to avoid what's inside because it appears easier. Yet in the end, inner contentment and peace come when we move past these inner stirrings and allow the calm deep within us to grow more fully.

THOUGHTS ON AGING PARENTS

I recently spoke with a friend of mine. I hadn't heard from him for a while and assumed that he was just working too many long hours or was spending lots of time with a romantic interest. To my surprise, my friend had been distant because he was preoccupied with family matters. His mother was diagnosed with cancer.

My friend lives at a distance from his parents. While my friend is a very successful guy, the process that led to his mother's diagnosis and movement to treatment has left him feeling very powerless. While he's been an advocate by phone to help his mother secure the medical appointments she needed on a timely basis, he found that there was little more that he could do.

As we spoke, he said to me, "I never understood what it was like for you with your father's illness. Sometimes you'd get really down, and I didn't understand why. I do now."

My father, who is in Pennsylvania, has lived with Parkinson's disease for many years. He's been bedridden because of the disease for about five years. It has been challenging to watch him slowly slip away.

One might say, "Well, you're not the one with the illness. Your parents need the help. You need to just get on with life." To be honest, some people have suggested that to me, especially when I was making one of my frequent trips back east. However, adult children of aging, infirm, or ill parents face a maze of emotions.

While we have known that our parents would one day die, the experience of having the strong elder who raised you grow weak brings home a different sense of life. Not only does it remind us of life's shortness, but it also causes us to reflect on our fragility.

Many adult children want to do whatever they can to assist their parents. But often, because of living at a distance, there is precious little that can be done. No matter what arrangements are made, one wrestles periodically with guilt over wanting to do more.

The guilt over wanting to do more just reinforces the powerlessness in the situation. While we are often powerless over many aspects of life, we generally prefer to live with the illusion that we are in control of our lives. When that illusion is seriously challenged, of course we become anxious.

For those who have unfinished business with our parents, dealing with their aging or illness is even more confusing. Perhaps we are angry over things done in the past. Perhaps the things done in the past were horrific, like physical or sexual abuse. I've worked with several people whose grief over the death of a parent was seriously complicated because of childhood abuse. It's understandable that when a person remains hurt and angry from childhood abuse, the individual may want to see the abuser suffer in some way. When the abuser is a parent for whom a child also has affection, the child—even an adult child—feels pulled apart.

The bottom line is that adult children of aging or infirm parents are often left with little support while facing confusing and complex issues. I don't have a solution for life's complexities. However, I believe it's important to name and understand the issues and have someone to talk to about them.

I was glad I was able to talk with my friend about his concerns with his mother. While we've been very good friends, something about the experience makes me feel closer to him. I was glad when the reports came back that the cancer had not spread. I sincerely hope that the surgery and chemotherapy will work effectively for her. While she experiences a roller coaster of emotions in this process, so do her family members. Yes, that roller coaster of emotions is very real. It's the way life is. Rather than deny the difficulty of life, we need to learn to accept that pain and confusion and find hope in the midst of it.

PART FOUR:
LESSONS FROM LIFE IN THE DESERT

DESERT SPIRITUALITY:
LEARNING FROM THE DRY HEAT

When I moved to the Desert Southwest, it was my hope to renew parts of me that seemed to have been lost over the last twelve years of busyness. During those twelve years, my life was simply too full for my own good.

While I lived in Tucson, I had the opportunity to pray, reflect, grapple with emotions, and write. The often-stark beauty of the Sonoran landscape and the dry heat of our climate challenged me to dig deep into myself and find wellsprings of refreshment. The process brought with it deep healing and intriguing challenges.

Living in desert country taught me important lessons. First, while the land is rugged and harsh, it is also very delicate. The balance of nature is finely tuned and easily upset. The delicate balance sustains life. The balance takes on unique beauty in the desert. The parched, dry land, with only a little rain, is quickly transformed into rich green life accented with colorful blossoms. So it is with us: there is a delicate balance that sustains our lives and can easily be upset. The balance includes the rough, rugged aspects of our lives. The rough, rugged parts are as much a part of the beauty of life as the peaceful and happy times. When our lives are parched, they are transformed to the new life of green and fresh blooms when watered with support and tenderness from others. That is essential to sustaining our well-being.

Yet it is not just what we receive from others that sustains us. Our rootedness in the depths of our being keeps us on course. This is the second lesson of the desert. As I drive through the desert, I am struck by the way lush trees grow in dry riverbeds and arroyos. Their roots have broken through into underground water that gives them life. Yes, there's plenty of water in this desert. The rivers run very deep, refreshing the heart of life. So it is for us. When we allow ourselves to be deeply rooted, we encounter the Source of Life within us. The Source will sustain us through the heat of the day, providing the refreshment we need even during the harshest times of our lives.

It's not only the deep running waters that bring us with clarity to the Source. The bright sun and the dry heat bleach those dead parts of life bare and enable us to appreciate the skeleton on which life took shape. That's the third lesson I've learned in the desert: the sun and the dry heat, from which we wisely shield ourselves with cotton clothes, hats, and sunscreen, will burn through to expose the framework that holds life together. As any student of anatomy knows, the life of the organism is integrated and brought to unity by its skeletal frame. Skeletons are usually hidden from view, sometimes in deep, dark closets. But the bright sun and dry heat of the desert strip bare the skeleton, allowing us to see what's really there. That's true for a dead carcass and true for the dead parts of our lives. The sun and dry heat will lay bare those joints and structures that hold us together so that we can better understand what is important for our lives.

These lessons are part of the unique spirituality of the desert. Yes, the desert, in its vastness and great diversity, has many lessons to teach. The question for us is always, "What am I open to learn?"

It's a Dry Heat

8:00 a.m. With cap on my head and water bottle in hand, I begin my morning walk in the park. Having just finished a half-hour of meditation, my mind and spirit are focused and alert. Following a sufficient intake of coffee, my body is also in gear. I enjoy this time to walk while doves coo, dogs run, and kids play on the swings.

Now that June has arrived, my morning walks are becoming more challenging. Just a few weeks ago, it was sixty-five degrees at this hour. Now, it's already over eighty degrees, and the sun is high enough in the sky to scorch the earth. I know it's reached the time of year to change my morning routine: walks will need to be much earlier so that I'm not wiped out before I begin my day.

There are many changes these days in Tucson. The traffic is lighter as snowbirds and students have left the desert. Tempers flare more quickly with the intensity of the afternoon heat. Swimming pools overflow with bodies splashing, hoping for a bit of cool in the midst of the heat. Many hope for a respite from the heat with an afternoon monsoon. But, hey, it's a dry heat, isn't it?

I find it amusing that the cliché so often used in the desert gives the impression that this "dry heat" is really no heat at all. On days when temperatures peak anywhere from 103 to 110, I especially laugh. I think to myself, *"Yeah, it's a dry heat," the dusty ol' codger gasped when collapsing in the desert from dehydration.*

Rather than bemoaning the heat, we learn to live with and move in it. The heat of the day invites us to slow down, rest, and be still. The changing weather patterns of hot sun and fierce monsoon rains invite us to re-collect our days and our pace. As roads wash out in the afternoon rains, we sometimes are faced with the problem: "I just can't get there from here."

Instead of stressing in the heat, we need to be wise enough to take time and rest. Allowing ourselves time and space to relax, share with friends, and reflect on life is a sacred opportunity the summer heat offers us. The brilliant, hot sun burns away all but what is essential. The sudden, powerful rains wash away the debris and clear the path up to the rocky summits. The sun and the rain can do these things not just in the Sonoran landscape but also in our lives, if we allow it to happen.

During the weeks of summer heat, nature provides us with the opportunity to slow down and take stock of what is essential in life. What is peripheral that can easily be put aside in the heat of life? Do you really need it? What debris is waiting to be washed away in a good, hard rain? What prevents the path of your life from being clear? Remember, too, that as the rain washes the debris clear, it also leaves new soil that is often rich in nutrients. What needs to be planted in this new soil of your life to enrich you?

Summer in the Sonoran Desert: yes, it's a time to reflect on what's most important in life, what's most important to live.

THE DESERT HEAT

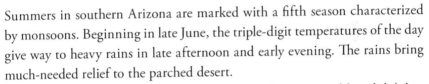

Summers in southern Arizona are marked with a fifth season characterized by monsoons. Beginning in late June, the triple-digit temperatures of the day give way to heavy rains in late afternoon and early evening. The rains bring much-needed relief to the parched desert.

One summer, the monsoons began earlier than expected but didn't last their usual six-week season. The much-needed rains dried up as quickly as they came. In that summer, southern Arizona baked in 100-plus temperatures each day. While clouds formed in the sky most afternoons, they were little more than a tease of what could be. No substantial rain fell for weeks.

Many of us survived the summer by insulating ourselves from the heat. I spoke with one person who was pleased to report that for more than two weeks she had not been outside of an air-conditioned environment. Insulation from the intensity of the midday sun and searing temperatures is but one way to deal with summer in the desert. I suspect some important life lessons can be gleaned from reflection on life in the Sonora.

The first peoples to inhabit the Sonoran Desert lived with a rhythm very different from our own. During the cooler winter months, native peoples lived in the Tucson valley, enjoying the temperate climate and vegetation. When the summer heat began to swell, these ancestors would head to the hills, spending their summers in the cooler heights of the mountains. At the first monsoon, there was a quick return to the valley to plant the crops that would be nourished by the summer rains while the community continued to live in the mountains. In autumn, people returned to the valley and enjoyed the harvest of Sonoran agriculture.

Once missionaries arrived in the valley, there were more year-round residents. The rhythm of life shifted from seasonal homes in the mountains to a daily routine that included an afternoon siesta. With shade and perhaps a breeze, the best option for an afternoon of 105-degree weather was to sleep.

Today, with the marvels of technology providing climate-controlled environments, we can simply pretend the heat isn't there. The weather has simply become a topic of conversation and little more than an occasional annoyance. But cool days and warm days are much the same for most of us. There's little change in our activities to accommodate the summer heat.

The heat of the desert summer is an apt metaphor for the difficult times of our lives. There are times when the challenges we encounter are scorching hot, when problems sear through us with a burning sensation, when things around us seem dry and lifeless. In these times, how do we respond? Do we pretend there's not a problem, attempting to live life as if all were cool and comfortable, just as though we're in air-conditioning that prevents us from experiencing the heat? Do we stick it out right where we are, getting through the worst of it by pulling back enough to recharge, taking psychological siestas to restore our stamina? Or do we create solutions and find ways to restore balance in inventive ways, much like those who learned to live both in the mountains and on the desert floor?

There are many ways to deal with the scorching heat life often brings our way. Pretending that the problems don't exist, much like living in a climate-controlled environment, prevents us from fully living our lives. Finding creative solutions to life's problems by living life with a sense of rhythm and balance opens us to the possibility of encountering life in all its fullness. Living with that sense of rhythm, maintaining the delicate inner balance, is among the important lessons to be gleaned from the desert heat.

LESSONS FROM THE PALO VERDE

As I walked through my neighborhood one evening, I couldn't help but notice the palo verde trees. These familiar trees of the Sonoran Desert are named for their green bark. Having no leaves, it's the green bark of the branches and trunk that do the work of photosynthesis: transforming the energy from sunlight and air, enabling the tree to breathe and be nourished.

Many of the palo verde trees in my neighborhood prune themselves. The palo verde does this work from an amazing instinct. When there is not enough water for the tree, the tree begins to prune itself, cutting off nutrients to specific branches. Most trees and other plants, when lacking sufficient water, begin to wither and die. But not the palo verde. The palo verde cuts back its own growth, losing a branch or two so that the rest of the tree can remain healthy. By this self-pruning, allowing a branch or two to die when there's not enough water to nourish the entire tree, the palo verde assures its own survival and healthy growth for many years, even in the dry desert climate.

As a professional psychologist and spiritual director, I work with many people who struggle to hold onto things in their lives that just don't work for them any longer. Many people carry old baggage such as hurts, scars, or habits that may have at one time had a positive role in their lives but are now no longer useful. Sometimes the old baggage was the best way that someone had to cope with a difficult situation. Now they use that coping mechanism to solve all kinds of unrelated problems. Other times, old baggage is like a trunk filled with hurt, anger, and resentment for things other people did years ago. All the old baggage does is weigh them down and make life's journey more difficult to travel.

Many of us use a great deal of energy to carry the old baggage around with us. Some of us know that we are very tired from lugging around the excess, yet are unwilling to give it up. We've grown used to it. It's familiar. It's become part of who we are. Yet the only way to grow more fully is to get rid of the baggage. Perhaps it needs to be put into storage; perhaps it needs to be taken to the garbage dump; perhaps it needs to be placed somewhere that it can be memorialized for what it was: something that may have helped in the past but whose usefulness is gone. However we understand the baggage, the important thing to realize is that carrying it with us only weighs us down and uses up essential resources that could be utilized for our growth.

The palo verde tree understands by instinct when there are too many branches to maintain its own health. It remedies the situation by pruning itself. By self-pruning, the tree is able to assure its own long and vital life. I suspect that many of us could learn some important lessons from the palo verde tree and recognize when it's time to let go of the things we can't maintain so that we can assure vitality and health for our future.

In the Shadow of the Saguaro

Before moving to Tucson, I read a great deal about the Sonoran Desert and its unique habitat. Of all the things I learned about, from coyotes to jumping cactus, perhaps the most thought-provoking lessons were from the saguaro. The saguaro cactus is the one thing that people picture most often from the Sonoran Desert. With stately arms reaching upward, the saguaro tower over the desert floor as a testament to life in our harsh climate.

The saguaro stands as a testament to commitment, patience, and careful growth. Our stately saguaros with grand arms have grown old with years. It takes an average of seventy-five years of slow growth for the first arm to appear. As I drive through the desert, seeing saguaros reaching up with four, five, and six arms, I wonder how long they have kept their patient vigil from their vistas.

Saguaros not only grow slowly, but they also die slowly. In the years when the Arizona cities were first developing suburban sprawl, saguaros were moved from the desert to be used as landscaping in yards. It took some time to realize that once a mature saguaro was moved, it dies. But its death march is slow, often taking eight or nine years to wither.

As a testament to patience, slow growth, and gradual decline, the saguaro stands as a reminder of the need to move through life with care and patience. Our tendency is to move through life at a hurried pace, rushing ahead to destinations that demand more of our time and energy. Driving across town, I often note cars weaving in and out of the lanes, trying to get ahead. I chuckle when I see those cars again, this time waiting at the same traffic light with me farther down the road. Living at the jostled pace of hurry-up-and-wait, the saguaros remind us to take time to take time. They have no need to hurry. They wait for the rains, growing slowly in spring and monsoon seasons. In the time it takes for a human being to live out its life course, the saguaro finally reaches up with the first arm, having rooted itself securely in the desert sands.

While they appear solitary in their stateliness, saguaros also know the rhythm of dependence and independence. A saguaro grows for the first years of its life under the shade of a mesquite tree. The mesquite provides shelter and shade for the young saguaro, softens the hard ground with its own expanse of roots, and helps to hold moisture in the ground. Because the saguaro grows so slowly, the mesquite completes its own life span before the saguaro's height competes with the mesquite. Without the mesquite, the young saguaro would not have the shelter to grow strong and tall.

As much as we don't want to admit it, we each need people in our lives who are like mesquite trees for us: people who provide shelter, shade, and protection for our own delicate growth. The heat of life's challenges and the dryness of life's trials can overwhelm any of us if left on our own. It is with the supportive care of others that we are enabled to grow healthy and strong, reaching out beyond ourselves, so that we too can provide shelter and safety to others. For that's indeed what the tall, old saguaro do.

Late in their lives, saguaros become home to Gila woodpeckers. The woodpeckers bore into the pulp of the saguaro, making nests between its ribs. These cool nesting places protect the woodpeckers from predators by providing homes beyond their reach. In time, woodpeckers move on, to be replaced by owls and purple martins, who find comfort and safety in the heart of the saguaros.

There is a rhythm to the life of the saguaro from receiving protection in its early life in the shade of the mesquite to providing cool shelter to birds in its later life. All the while, the saguaro grows at a slow steady pace, standing tall as a testament to the abundance of life in the desert.

PART FIVE:
LESSONS FOR THE HOLIDAYS

New Year's: A Second Chance

I remember reading somewhere that in some villages in Italy people celebrate New Year's by throwing things (including furniture and heavy objects) out of windows into the streets. I recall that this is to mark a new beginning by letting go of the past. I've never celebrated New Year's with that level of gusto. But I quickly got beyond my youthful experience of New Year's Eve spent in a monastery. In that particular monastery, at midnight, some monks jingled their rosary beads outside their bedroom doors. I suppose they were the handiest noisemakers available.

Tending to be a bit conventional, my New Year celebrations include neither throwing furniture nor jingling rosaries. No matter how one celebrates New Year's Eve, I do think that the new year provides a special opportunity to reflect on our lives, looking ahead to the future.

Many people make New Year's resolutions. Often, they are the same resolutions each year: eat less, work out more, get a new job, or find the perfect mate. It seems that most people do well if they keep these resolutions for a few weeks or so. I suspect that they rarely make it past mid-January.

Perhaps part of the problem with New Year's resolutions is that they tend to be external changes. We decide we want to change something we do and decide to do it by willpower.

When I explain hypnosis to my clients, I talk about using willpower to make behavioral changes. Willpower is sort of like mental adrenaline. As adrenaline gives us a boost of energy to make it through some strenuous activity, so willpower gives us a boost to make behavioral changes. Both adrenaline and willpower only work in the short term. For real physical competency, we need training to perform at our peak levels. Physical training requires time and work. Taking time and work to accomplish a goal is something many people would prefer to skip. That's true whether we are aiming to meet physical, psychological, or spiritual goals.

The tradition of making New Year's resolutions has wisdom in it. As we begin a calendar year, we begin a new cycle of our lives. We are given the opportunity to consider and assess the quality of our lives and how we can make changes for our own good. Sometimes we need the help of others to make that assessment and understand what changes are appropriate. Most of the time, the changes won't occur by using our willpower. That's because real change happens inside of us. It's only after making an internal shift in our perspective that our external behavior changes.

Rather than making the same old resolutions each new year, perhaps we would do something more beneficial for ourselves if we took the time to consider what's important in our lives. Once we have completed this kind of self-assessment, we are in a position to make the internal shifts necessary to live in accordance with what is important to us. This requires that we consider the values we hold as important to us and allow these values to be the basis of our actions.

Many people find it difficult to make such changes alone. Good friends and skilled counselors can help a great deal in the process. They assist us in recognizing the forest from the trees of our lives. Having a clearer perspective, we are then able to take steps on the path we know is right for us.

While it's easier to make a few quick resolutions again this new year, those who really want to improve the quality of their lives aren't afraid of doing some extra work. Doing so results in greater satisfaction in life rather than frustration over unkept resolutions in just a few weeks.

EASTER: A BOLD CELEBRATION

Easter: a celebration of new life and renewed hope. Or at least that's what I think Easter is.

I ate at a fast-food restaurant for lunch today. The windows and counters were covered with cardboard cutouts of pastel-colored bunnies and eggs and other cute springlike decorations of various shapes and sizes. To be honest, the decor was not exactly enticing to my aesthetic appreciation. At best, I could say that it was sort of cute. As happens to me at other holidays, I looked at the decorations and was left feeling as though this important celebration was relegated to something pretty for children. Can Easter have meaning for adults in our secular age?

While I am sure that some readers expect me to wax eloquently about the importance of Easter within a Christian context, that is not the purpose of this column. Those will be the reflections I include in the sermon I will preach on Easter Sunday at church. Instead, I wonder if we have become too jaded to be able to celebrate life and look for hope in the world today.

As gay and lesbian people, many of us have faced a great deal of trauma in life. In fact, I doubt that most of us realize the amount of pain we have experienced in life. Because of violence, HIV/AIDS, addictions, unsuccessful relationships, unfulfilling jobs, and a host of other problems in life, many of us have become numb to life around us. The challenges we face in life are magnified by the larger problems of our society, including racism, sexism, homophobia, and classism. Many people live just a paycheck or two from financial disaster. Others struggle with feelings of loneliness, isolation, and inadequacy. Complaints of boredom or lack of motivation are common because it is so difficult for us to engage ourselves creatively in life. Perhaps in the midst of all of life's problems and challenges, many of us feel like there really is nothing to celebrate.

I would insist that it is because at least from time to time the struggles and tensions of life seem overwhelming for many of us that the celebration of Easter is so important. The celebration of the Easter holiday, whether secular or sacred, is a statement of faith that even with all life's problems and challenges, life can be renewed. Yes, even in the darkest moments in life, Easter insists that hope can be found.

The renewal of Easter acknowledges that reality in the world around us. It affirms that just as seemingly dead bulbs burst into colorful flowers, just as the cycle of winter's harshness breaks into spring's gentle beauty, just as our animal friends innately continue to create new life, so too, we humans have the ability to create new life and hope for ourselves. Yes, even in the midst of life's greatest challenges, the possibility of hope can be found.

Easter is much more than a children's holiday. If we allow Easter to be nothing more than something pretty for kids, then we miss the opportunity to take a step beyond the limitations that life presents to all of us and boldly grasp the fullness of life that is meant to be savored and celebrated.

On Thanksgiving:
The Great Mystery of Beauty

For the beauty of the earth;
For the glory of the skies;
For the love that from our birth
Over and around us lies!
God of all, to you we raise
This our song of grateful praise!

And so we sang the hymn for the opening of a service I attended in the Black Hills, Rapid City, South Dakota. I was asked to speak there, visiting a congregation I'd become fond of over the years. It was good to again see some of the familiar faces from my last visit a few years earlier.

Spending time with an old friend who lives in the area, worshipping on Sunday with that congregation, and taking time to drive and hike in the Black Hills of South Dakota gave me an opportunity to pause and be thankful.

South Dakota is a place that has a certain romance for me. The Native American tradition that I learned about first was the culture of the Lakota. The Lakota ancestral home is the Black Hills. They are people of the Plains who hunted buffalo and believe in the Great Mystery that animates all life. That Great Mystery is reverenced through the way of life Lakota peoples still live.

Sitting on a downed tree in the Black Hills, watching deer to my left

---

* Pierpoint, Folliott S. "For the Beauty of the Earth," first published in 1864 in a book of poems entitled *The Sacrifice of Praise;* now in public domain.

feeding on the autumn brown grass, aware of the three buffalo that were not far from me on my right, I reflected on the balance and beauty of life that is woven in such an awe-inspiring mystery. While science interprets the clues to our origins on this planet and religious traditions provide a context of meaning for life, in truth it is mystery that holds the cosmos together and orders the passing of days and seasons. It is a marvelous mystery.

Returning home to Arizona, I encounter that same mystery in life around me. The Navajo people, the Diné, understand the binding force in a way very different from the Lakota. For the Diné, beauty is around us, within us, over us, behind us, in front of us, and below us. It is in beauty that the Diné walk the path of life, no matter where that path leads. To speak of beauty is not a matter of physical appearance or a quality of aesthetic appreciation. Instead, it is the quality of balance and our ability to live in communion with the balance that holds all life together that the Diné reverence and respect.

In celebrating Thanksgiving, the spirituality found in the land inspires me to reflect on the mystery that is the source and binding force of life. As I encounter that Great Mystery, I find that I can do nothing but stand in awe at its beauty. My visit to Rapid City gave me the opportunity to begin my Thanksgiving observance early and to savor it. Savoring gratitude for life is perhaps something sweeter than homemade pumpkin pie!

THANKS GIVEN FOR LIFE

It's one of those memories that is very clear in my mind. I must have been only eight or nine years old at the time. I lay in bed one evening, all snug and warm under the blankets. Before going to sleep, I counted my blessings one by one. I don't remember the total number, but I'm pretty sure that I ran out of fingers and toes. Just like my teacher told us to do that day before school recessed for the long holiday weekend, I went to sleep counting all my blessings and the things for which I had reason to be thankful.

Giving thanks for what we have received—that is the purpose of the holiday we celebrate in late November. It is only the United States and Canada that have a holiday dedicated to "thanks-giving." We all know that this celebration is traced to the harvest feast celebrated by the Pilgrims, a celebration they learned from their Native American neighbors in the 1600s.

After a few horrible years of barely surviving in their new home, with many dying in the harsh New England climate, the colonists slowly learned to adapt to their new environment. They watched how their Native neighbors planted the three sisters with care: corn, beans, and squash. They adapted to hunting and preserving new kinds of game and learned from painful experience what was necessary to survive in the short growing season and the long, cold winters. Through the tough lessons life taught them, they learned to give thanks.

While images of that first Thanksgiving, with Pilgrims and Indians gathered around one table, are little more than a poetic retelling of actual events, the Pilgrims seemed to have learned an important lesson from the first residents of their new home: the communal nature of giving thanks.

In most Native American cultures, following a good harvest or a profitable hunt, a village feast occurred. All shared equally in the feast, no matter what role one played in providing the meal. It was unthinkable to not share the bounty of the harvest or hunt, because the bounty was truly a gift received. Recognizing the generosity of the land and the four-legged and winged creatures who gave their lives to sustain human life, Native villages knew they had much to be thankful for.

As human life has moved away from this simple dependence of living on Mother Earth, we have lost this original sense of Thanksgiving. Few of us have experienced life as lived in a balance, not being sure who would live through the winter, hoping that the harvest would be sufficient to feed our families, wondering whether our skills as hunters would enable us to bring home the bacon or turkey or venison. The thanks given in these celebrations were thanks to have made it through when the odds seemed so great and positive outcomes seemed so unclear.

While the lessons of thanksgiving I was taught as a child helped me understand the importance of this feast, the tradition of giving thanks is much richer than remembering our momentary successes in life. The tradition of giving thanks is an act of remembering that our lives are dependent on forces beyond us. Yes, each of us is here today because of a gracious design of life that provides the opportunity for our survival. It is that foundational realization that is the cause of our giving thanks.

From this perspective, many of us can find reason to be truly thankful on this holiday, thankful for being able to make it through the hurdles of life. There are those who would not be with us if it weren't for the advances in treatment of HIV. There are others who have come close to choosing death because they felt such deep despair because family and friends would not accept them for the people they were created to be. There are those who have experienced fear and dread from violence at home or school and in our streets. There are still others who are thankful for the generosity of unknown benefactors who provide food and shelter from the cold.

As we celebrate the Thanksgiving holiday, let us truly be thankful for the opportunity to be here and celebrate the feast. It is indeed a gracious gift.

WAITING: PART OF CHRISTMAS PREPARATION

The lines in the stores get longer. The traffic is heavier. The list of things to do never seems to end. It's as if every step on our way is interrupted. Time seems wasted as we wait.

There's no escaping it. We look for the shortest line at the store. We think through our route before driving it. We check for any opportunity to get ahead. There are so many things to do. Time still seems to be wasted as we wait.

The Christmas season is filled with so many good things. We give gifts to our loved ones, showing them we care. We gather with friends to celebrate, tell stories, laugh, and share. We send greetings to those in distant places, including letters about the changes in our lives over this past year. We decorate our homes, offices, and yes, even our cars, to help celebrate the season with joy. Yet we are often frustrated, even angered, when in the midst of all our special holiday preparations, we are forced to stop and wait.

Waiting. It's such a basic human experience. Yet in our fast-paced society, many of us find waiting a horrible experience. We want things fast: fast food, high-speed Internet connections, real-time communication, and instant service. We reward those most able to "multitask" in their jobs and expect that we should all be proficient at handling many things at once. Waiting disturbs us. It doesn't fit our values, our priorities, and our expectations.

In truth, waiting is an essential human experience. It is an experience of anticipation, desire, and longing for that which satisfies us.

Think of waiting in a restaurant for a loved one to arrive. The minutes pass slowly. Time almost stands still. We wonder, tensely, about the beloved's delay. All of that fades in an instant when the beloved arrives. There's a sense of relief, fulfillment, relaxation, and happiness at the arrival of the beloved. Time is experienced in a new way.

The rhythm of waiting and fulfillment is an essential human experience. A mother waits nine months for the birth of her child; the farmer waits through the growing season for the crop to mature; we wait, hope, anticipate so many of life's experiences, yet rarely learn to accept the rhythm between waiting and fulfillment that is part of the fabric of life.

Allowing ourselves to wait, to wait patiently, is to suspend our own sense of priority. Waiting is an opportunity to discover ourselves in the context of others. To wait calmly is to accept that we are not the most important being in the world, that it's really not all about me. Waiting allows us to discover ourselves in the context of others and admit that the fulfillment of our hopes and dreams depends not only on us but on others.

In these last days before Christmas, when you find yourself frustrated by waiting, remember that there is a lesson in the wait: the fulfillment we each seek in life isn't just about us; it is a matter of finding ourselves in the context of others. Waiting suspends our own agenda and gives us the opportunity to include others in the expectation of our own fulfillment.

Light in the Darkness

The candles of the menorah burned brightly during the eight days of Hanukkah. Electric stars and twinkling lights illuminate Christmas trees. In but a few days, new candles will be kindled for Kwanza celebrations. We must not forget those of Native and earth-centered traditions who dance, sing, and drum during these days of Winter Solstice. As the daylight has grown shorter and night longer, our festive celebrations of this special season share a common theme: light shines in the darkness.

My spiritual roots are in the Eastern Christian tradition. The rituals and holidays of my background are somewhat different from those of many other people. The celebration of Christmas Eve is an important memory that still nurtures my reflections: in the darkened church, an icon is brought out while people sing the antiphon: "Emmanuel! God is with us!"

The icon is a rendering of the birth of the Christ Child. The picture is much different from the depictions in Western traditions. In the icon, the image is of a birth in the recesses of a dark cave. The single beam of light from a star illuminates the cave. The underlying message is clear: light shines in the darkness.

Living our modern lives, the images of light and darkness have little impact on us. After all, if we want light, we flick a switch and there is light. Even outdoors, electric illumination is available with just a little effort on our part. But in a different time, in the centuries that nurtured the spiritual traditions we learn from today, life revolved around the clear cycle of day and night. Without the sun illuminating the day, the darkness of night became a time to be close to home. Travel at night was dangerous. Night predators had the advantage. The ancient images of night are mostly images of fear, danger, and great difficulty. Light in the darkness was a precious gift.

While we rarely label it as such, darkness is an apt metaphor for many parts of our life. While images of the dark side make us think of *Star Wars* and Darth Vader, the dark sides of our lives are parts of us that often cause us great anguish. We find that anger and resentment, self-doubt and shame, often eat away at us and come out at times when they are least expected. We struggle with worries and fears for the future, wondering if there will be money to pay bills, fretting about finding love, or anxious about our jobs and careers. Many in our community dull the pain of inner darkness with addictions to alcohol, drugs, and sex. Yet the pain remains, only wearing a mask.

The message of this holiday season is not one of trite sentiment and greetings. No, the message is one of profound hope: light shines in the darkness. And the darkness will not overcome the light.

Our spiritual traditions teach us to have hope in the possibility of a new beginning. That new beginning may be symbolized in the lighting of a candle, the birth of a child, or the watching for sunrise at the solstice. But there is an underlying belief in the possibility of a brighter tomorrow.

What our spiritual traditions teach us is that no matter what the obstacles, the human spirit is resilient. There is a divine spark within each of us that, when properly nurtured, grows to a flame that warms and illuminates us, even in the midst of the darkest moments of life. But that illumination doesn't just happen. It occurs when we make the decisions and take the steps necessary to move into the light.

And so, during these holiday celebrations, as we enjoy the company of family and friends, we have the opportunity to find the courage to allow light to grow in our lives so that the pain we each carry deep within can be healed. Indeed, light shines in the darkness.

LED BY A LITTLE CHILD

While preparing to celebrate Christmas this weekend, I've thought a great deal about what this holiday means to me. It's probably not surprising that I'd reflect on the images of the Judeo-Christian scriptures during this season.

This year, one image in particular struck me in a new way. It's from the Hebrew prophet Isaiah, chapter 11. I suspect it's familiar to many people:

> *The wolf will live with the lamb,*
> *The leopard will lie down with the newborn lamb;*
> *The calf and the lion will graze together,*
> *And a little child will lead them.*
> (paraphrase of text my own)

The prophet is looking to the day when a new world order replaces the competition, tyranny, and injustice that are all-too-familiar in life as we know it. In the new world order, natural enemies will live in harmony with each other, and a little child will lead them.

While Christians clearly interpret this passage as referring to the birth of the Christ Child, as I read this passage I thought of a visit with good friends of mine and my godson, Tanner. Tanner is a bright and bouncy four-year-old, the child of two lesbian friends who live in another part of the country. My friends have been a couple for more than twelve years. Several years ago, they began learning about artificial insemination and the challenges lesbian parents face. Eventually, Tanner came along.

As we live in distant parts of the country, I only get to see them about once a year. At each visit, Tanner is almost like a new person. I remember visiting when Tanner was at that stage when he was able to walk well enough on his own to bolt from one place to the next. He would go from one toy to another, stop, and squeal with delight. He'd look around at whoever was there, almost as if to say, "Hey! Look what I found! Isn't this great!" He would go to the next thing, stop, squeal, and look for someone to join in.

"And a little child will lead them."

What would it really be like to be led through life like a little child? I think about Tanner's rushing from toy to toy, stopping to express his delight. I imagine encountering life like a little child, filled with that level of joy and delight at everything that happens to be in my path. Yes, if we allowed ourselves to be led by the enthusiasm of a little child, it would be a new world order. We would learn to savor the unique gift that is life and appreciate the sheer goodness found in the things around us.

At Christmas, we remember the birth of a child. We celebrate by giving gifts. We sing carols proclaiming peace on earth. But the real spirit of Christmas will be ours when we open ourselves to be led by that little child that is still in each one of us.

Epilogue

On June 1, 2004, with my belongings packed into a moving van, I began to drive across country heading to the east. Leaving Tucson, Arizona, behind, I was beginning a new chapter in my life. Over the years in Tucson, I was enchanted with the desert vistas, experienced wonder at night skies dancing with luminaries, and was overcome by the power of lightning storms in the midst of summer heat. My life crossed the paths of many others. I also left something of myself from my work teaching, doing therapy, and pasturing a small congregation.

As I drove east on Interstate 10, I recalled the first time I drove the route when moving to southern Arizona. In 1997, I traveled alone, with vague hopes for the future. Over my years in the desert, my sense of myself and my focus in life changed. By many standards, I still lived a busy life. But even in the midst of many endeavors, I learned to maintain a simpler focus in life and to live with a greater sense of mindfulness.

Other things had also changed. Moving from Tucson, I traveled with my life partner, Kin, whom I had met in Tucson. After living for many years with Parkinson's disease, my father had passed. This move back across the country was based on my mother's need for more care as her life became more fragile.

I have very fond memories of my years in Tucson. The things that shaped my life most during my years in the desert were the rhythm of prayer and meditation I found at the monastery of the Benedictine Sisters of Perpetual Adoration, the pace of walks each morning that helped me to greet the day, and the depth of the subtle yet bold spiritual teacher the Sonoran Desert proved to be. The lessons I stumbled into over my years in Tucson are lessons that have significantly impacted my life. I believe that these lessons will continue to shape my life.

Perhaps there is something from my reflections on life in Tucson that will inspire insights for you as a reader. Yet I recognize that we each have our own path to follow. Because of that recognition, I wish you well as you stumble into your own life's lessons. Savor the path you follow. Look for inspiration on each step of the journey. There is no doubt that you will find many things to learn along the way.

About the Author

The Reverend Dr. Louis F. Kavar is an experienced therapist, spiritual director, minister, and professor of psychology. Throughout his career, Dr. Kavar has worked with individuals, groups, and organizations in the area of spirituality. He has led retreats, taught classes, and presented seminars throughout the United States, Canada, Mexico, England, Australia, and New Zealand. His relaxed manner and use of humor make him an exceptional and accessible presenter in the area of spirituality.

Dr. Kavar holds a master of arts degree in spirituality from Duquesne University and a PhD in counseling from the University of Pittsburgh.

An ordained minister in the United Church of Christ, Dr. Kavar has over thirty years of experience in working with individuals and groups in the areas of personal and spiritual development. Dr. Kavar teaches in the doctoral program in psychology at the Harold Abel School of Social and Behavioral Sciences at Capella University, an online learning environment. He lives in St. Louis with his partner, Kin Lo.

Dr. Kavar previously lived in Tucson, Arizona, where he was the director of Desert Vision Counseling and Hypnotherapy, a private practice specializing in issues of spirituality, wholeness, and creativity. He was also among the faculty and design team for the Hesychia School of Spiritual Direction.

When a resident of Miami, Dr. Kavar was the clinical director for South Florida's Pastoral Care Network. Headquartered at the United Protestant Appeal, this program provided spiritually based counseling to people living with chronic illnesses and their loved ones in a three-county region. He was also preceptor for spiritual care in a residency program at the University of Miami's Department of Psychiatry.

About the Illustrator

Patricia Chase Bergen is an artist living in Tucson, Arizona. Her work in bronze, watercolor, and other media can be found in galleries in southern Arizona.

Recommended Resources

The following books explore the spiritual practices discussed in *Stumbling into Life's Lessons,* as well as life in the Sonoran Desert.

Alcock, John. *Sonoran Desert Spring.* Tucson: University of Arizona Press, 1994.

Blythe, Teresa. *50 Ways to Pray: Practices from Many Traditions and Times.* Nashville: Abingdon Press, 2006.

Brother Lawrence. *Practice the Presence of God: New Revised Version in Modern English* (Jim Johnson, Tr.). San Jose: Reset Publishing, an Imprint of JC Media Publishing, 2009.

Cepero, Helen. *Journaling as a Spiritual Practice: Encountering God Through Attentive Writing.* Downers Grove: IVP Books, 2008.

Gunaratana, Bhante Henepola. *Mindfulness in Plain English.* Boston: Wisdom Publications, 2002.

Nabhan, Gary Paul. *The Desert Smells Like Rain: A Naturalist in O'odham Country.* Tucson: University of Arizona Press, 2002.

Pennington, Basil. *Centering Prayer: Renewing an Ancient Christian Prayer Form.* New York: Image Press, 1982.

Peterson, Eugene H. *Eat This Book: A Conversation in the Art of Spiritual Reading.* Grand Rapids: Wm. B. Eerdmans Publishing Company, 2009.

Phillips, Steven J., and Patricia Wentworth Comus, Eds. *A Natural History of the Sonoran Desert.* Berkley: University of California Press/ASDM Press, 1999.

Phillips, Susan S. *Candlelight: Illuminating the Art of Spiritual Direction.* Harrisburg: Morehouse Publishing, 2008.

Vest, Norvene. *Tending the Holy: Spiritual Direction Across Traditions.* Harrisburg: Morehouse Publishing, 2003.

As you stumble into your own life's lessons, join the discussion with other readers at <u>www.loukavar.com</u>. While there, you can download e-books and find a community of people sharing spiritual exploration.